GUNNAR JOHNSON

Generous
LIFE JOURNEY
THE ROAD TO FINANCIAL FREEDOM

ENDORSEMENTS

Too often, when someone hears the word "stewardship" at church, they immediately grab their wallets and think, "*Here it comes. The church is after my money again!*" That's a tragic misunderstanding of the biblical principles of stewardship. A steward is just a manager of God's resources! In *Generous Life Journey*, Gunnar Johnson draws on years of research and hands-on ministry to unpack true, biblical stewardship. What you learn just might change your life!

~ Dave Ramsey
New York Times best-selling author and nationally syndicated radio show host

If you're thinking this is just another book about tithing, let me assure you—what God has given Gunnar Johnson to share with those who desire more in their lives and in their churches is greater than anything you've probably been given before. With practical applications, valuable tips, godly wisdom and insight, Gunnar has written a book that encompasses all aspects of your life and helps you discover what you're supposed to be doing and all God has for you. Gunnar says life with God is an adventure and his encouragement to us is: "Let the adventure begin!"

~ John C. Maxwell
Best-selling author, leadership expert, Founder of EQUIP International

I've had the privilege of walking with Gunnar Johnson on his personal generosity path over the last ten years. His success story is very simple: he listened to God and obeyed. You will be encouraged in your own journey by learning more of his!

~ Sharon Epps
Partner, Women Doing Well

It has been my privilege to consult with and coach leaders from some of the most effective churches in America, and there is no doubt that Gunnar Johnson is truly one of the good guys. His work at Gateway Church has been a model for so many of us who are working to inspire generosity, stewardship and giving. I am confident that wisdom in his new book will help countless Christ-followers find the financial freedom the Lord wants for each of us.

~ Chris Willard
Co-author *of Contagious Generosity, Creating a Culture of Giving in Your Church*, Director of Generosity Initiatives, Leadership Network and Generosity Strategist, Generis

I have had the privilege of watching Gunnar Johnson develop into one of America's leading Stewardship Pastors. He speaks with experience and authority. He is a person who walks his talk personally, but more than that, he is able to communicate what he knows in a compelling and transferable way. I recommend this book heartily.

~ Ron Blue
Founding Director, Kingdom Advisors

Gunnar Johnson's own journey to a generous life qualifies him as a very capable guide! Read the book and put God's principles into action.

~ Chuck Bentley
CEO, Crown Financial Ministries

Gunnar Johnson teaches us that financial problems are really spiritual problems. The secret of financial freedom is really a "heart issue." This book is biblical, yet practical. It's hard hitting, yet easy to read as he takes us on his own personal journey from bondage to mammon toward financial freedom.

~ Wayne Hilsden
Lead Pastor, King of Kings Community, Jerusalem

TABLE OF CONTENTS

ACKNOWLEDGMENTS

I am the product of a loving Savior, Christ Jesus, and great family, friends and mentors.

For your unconditional love as we live this adventure, I would like to thank my wife, Missy, and my kids, Faith, Katelyn and Elijah. My parents, Curtis Johnson and Melynda Bonner, as well as my in-laws, Steve and Debbie Mathews, have all been a priceless source of wisdom and encouragement.

A special "thank you" goes to my Senior Pastor, Robert Morris, for teaching me so much about generosity, stewardship and modeling godly leadership. And also to my Gateway Church oversights: Tom Lane, Todd Lane and Kevin Grove who have helped me weave stewardship ministry into a growing local church body.

God has blessed me with some amazing mentors who taught me, encouraged me and modeled Biblical stewardship: Dale Brooks, Sharon Epps, Chuck Missler, Chuck Bentley, Dave Ramsey, Howard Dayton, Ron Blue, Patrick Johnson, Chris Goulard, Dave Briggs, Jerry Schriver and Dick Towner.

To the most amazing Gateway Church stewardship team who have tirelessly put feet to the ministry vision: Leo Sabo, Kiasi Valentine, James Morris, Chad Sykes, Mashelle James and Yoana Sampayo as well as our incredible volunteer team.

Thank you to my close friends and prayer team: Tobey and Marsia Van Wormer, Mark and Misti Presley, Dustin Parker, Daniel Rowland, Ron Brooks, Martin Day, Mark Mueller, Zach Neese and Geoff Cohen.

And thank you to those who helped me get my teaching on paper: Henry McLaughlin, my editor Joyce Freeman, Bobby Williams and the Create team, and the never-out-of-energy or laughs, my Project Manager, Marsia Van Wormer.

FOREWORD

It may be the oldest concept in the Word of God. It was certainly at the root of Earth's first family's very first assignment. And it was a failure in this area that plunged the world and all humanity into darkness, scarcity and death.

I'm talking about *stewardship*.

God put Adam and Eve in a place of abundance and gave them instructions to "cultivate and keep" it (Genesis 2:15). That's a stewardship assignment. A loving Father encouraged them to eat freely of every amazing tree in that amazing garden. Any and all—except one. One tree was to be left untouched. Unconsumed.

That, too, was a stewardship assignment. Faithful stewards don't consume for themselves what a generous, holy God says is to be His and His alone.

God's plan always was and still is for us to enjoy abundance through stewardship and generosity. And when Jesus, the Last Adam, came and made right everything the First Adam had messed up, that kind of blessing and joy became possible once more.

Now, as it was back then, the key concept is stewardship.

Cultivating a lifestyle of generosity is a very personal subject for me. Before my life was completely transformed by an encounter with Jesus Christ, I was chronically selfish, proud and materialistic. When God's love took hold of me, it turned a self-centered and self-destructive young man into someone very different.

When, at the age of 19 in a shabby little motel room, I got saved, the first thing I wanted to do was give. I wanted to give to everyone I could. I wanted to bless others and help them know what I had found. Why? Gratitude. I was just unspeakably grateful for the forgiveness, freedom, peace and purpose I found in God's gift of Jesus.

That was many years ago. As a pastor over the last several decades, I've encountered countless precious couples and individuals who love God and belong to Him—and yet are not experiencing any of the blessing, joy and peace Jesus died to make available to them. In fact, most Christians in our culture are suffering from the very same financial diseases as those who don't know God.

It's an epidemic in our culture. A 2013 study by a banking organization revealed that 76% of America's households are living paycheck-to-paycheck. And a full 50% of us have less than a three-month cushion of living expenses in savings. More than 25% had no savings at all! An appalling number of people are essentially drowning in debt.

It's one thing for people who do not know God—those who have not been delivered from the enemy's grasp at the cost of Jesus' very blood—to live this way. But for God's redeemed people to do so is a tragedy. An unnecessary tragedy.

That is why teaching people to live blessed lives by following God's principles of faithful stewardship has been a core part of our mission of Gateway Church from its first day of existence. I'm convinced the reason we have been so blessed as a church is that we have endeavored to not only teach these truths but to follow them.

We just keep endeavoring to be good stewards with what God gives us, and He just keeps entrusting us with more.

That brings me to the book you now hold in your hands. I believe it is very much a key to a better life for you and your family. A blessed life.

Years ago the elders of Gateway Church recognized that ministering to people in the area of financial freedom and stewardship would require more than just periodic teaching from the pulpit. We saw that people not only needed to understand the spiritual principles and precepts of stewardship, but needed practical, specific help in areas such as budgeting, debt elimination strategies, priority setting and much more.

We established an entire department dedicated to helping our members walk out powerful, practical, biblical solutions to their financial challenges. And Gunnar Johnson has been instrumental in carrying out and growing this vision from the beginning.

Over the years I've watched Gunnar personally walk hundreds of couples and single parents step-by-step out of the dark financial forests in which they thought they were hopelessly trapped—guiding them into the bright sunshine of financial freedom and blessing. I can't think of any individual better equipped to help you make the same journey to blessing.

I'm excited for you to grasp the truths Gunnar shares on the following pages, because I have a powerful passion for seeing God's people walking in all the blessing and kingdom effectiveness that result from a lifestyle of generosity.

Nothing gives me more joy than to see people stepping out and stepping up to this kind of life. Not "giving to get." Giving to honor God. Giving out of gratitude to Jesus. Giving to break the hold of the spirit of Mammon. And being abundantly blessed—not just in their finances but in every area of their lives—as a result.

You're in good hands. My prayer is that you'll open your heart and your mind to the concepts you'll find here. And that as you do, you'll find the courage to embark on the exciting, rewarding journey of living a generous life.

~Robert Morris
Senior and Founding Pastor, Gateway Church

INTRODUCTION

Did you ever dream of winning the lottery and what you would do with all that money? Pay off your debt? Build your dream house? Pay off your parents' or your in-laws' debts?

Well, I don't play the lottery, but I have to confess, on a few occasions, I have thought about my game plan if I did win.

A few years ago, my wife, Missy, asked me a similar question: *"If money was no object, what would you do?"* That question sent me into several months of prayer to figure it out.

Fast forward about ten years and, today, I am blessed to be doing my dream job: Pouring my life into my home church and connecting with other churches, training leaders to lead stewardship ministries and teaching people how to become free both spiritually and with money, and showing them how to live what God created them for from the beginning of time. I get to serve God's people, helping them to make their lives better.

Many mornings, I have to pinch myself to see if this is a dream or reality! The desire in my heart is to equip you to maximize your life in God's Kingdom. If I am successful in loving and teaching people God's Word about generosity and money, then I have accomplished my calling.

The purpose of this book is to teach you how to be financially free, how to fulfill the plan God has for your life, how to be a blessing to the Body of Christ and how to live a blessed life. This is a simple book explaining what the Bible says about money and how to actually live it.

In each chapter, I'm going to lay a firm Biblical foundation for the principles I'll cover. If I can talk you into believing something with just the persuasion of my own words, someone else can talk you out of it. But if you see it for yourself grounded in the Word of God, it will become a conviction.

Acts 17:11 reminds us of the people of Berea, who, when they heard Paul and Silas, *"listened with all readiness but they searched the scriptures daily to find out whether these things were true."* Anytime you hear something taught about money, be like Bereans—go to the Word and check it out!

A lot of junk about finances has been preached, and people in the Body of Christ have been hurt and wounded. As a church leader, I apologize for that hurt, and I ask for your forgiveness for the way well-intended, but misguided, clergy have taught generosity and finances in the past. Please take a moment and hit the "reset" button on what you've heard about finances.

Let's start with a clean slate.

I want to get you re-rooted in the Word in the area of finances. When you see it in the Word of God, the power of the Holy Spirit will transform your life!

CHAPTER ONE

THE BEGINNING

*"I'll prove this tithing doesn't work. I'll tithe my way into bankruptcy. God does **not** work in our finances in this modern day and age."*

At twenty-three-years-old, newly back walking with the Lord, I thought I knew everything. I wrestled with Malachi 3, with bringing the tithe to the storehouse and watching God open the windows of heaven over me. I didn't see it in my life, and I set out to prove the Bible wrong. I began tithing, but there was no faith in it. I was testing, seeking to prove my friend who challenged me about tithing, and the Word of God, wrong.

Change began to happen. I could see results—slowly, but they were coming.

My journey to this point had been a meandering path. I grew up in church. Mom served on the worship team, and Dad was very involved in a lot of church functions. It was a large and growing church so there was always something going on. My parents worked hard to be able to send me to a private Christian school. Being in church and around Jesus was second nature to me.

Then disaster struck. While I was in the eighth grade, my parents divorced, and I didn't see it coming and didn't handle it well. Over time, my parents had just grown apart from each other. Later, when Mom decided to remarry, I moved out because I didn't like my stepfather-to-be or his violent temper.

I went back and forth between Mom and Dad as the mood and home atmosphere hit me. Dad had the easier rules. There were only two: stay out of his hair and don't smoke in the house.

Without rules, I became more adventurous and began living from place to place. Mom, Dad, friends. Through it all, I always found a way to land on my feet. I worked at a movie theater at night and mowed lawns during the day. By the time I was fifteen, I owned a cool 1978 Honda 750 motorcycle and a customized 1967 Ford Econoline van. I ran with a rough crowd. Playing basketball was all that kept me out of big trouble.

At seventeen, I went back to church for the reason most guys go to church at that age—because that's where all the hot girls go on the weekend.

As I sat in the services, the Word of God slowly broke through my tough guy barriers and attitudes, chipping away at the wall around my heart. My brokenness was exposed, and I realized how much I was hurting, how much I needed my Savior. I had a revelation: My love for adventure was placed there by a God of adventure—Jesus.

During this time of searching for my foundation in Jesus, a co-worker at the movie theater challenged me to read Josh McDowell's *Evidence that Demands a Verdict*. I've always been one to question and challenge and search the Scriptures for answers. God used this

> My love for adventure was placed there by a God of adventure—Jesus

intellectual bent to draw me closer to Christ, and I accepted Him as my Savior on October 17, 1993.

And my life turned—not all at once, but it turned.

One of the elders of the church arranged for me to go back to the Christian academy I'd previously attended. I worked jobs before and after my classes and still had time to play basketball for the school, making first team All State and MVP in our division in 1994.

God began to equip me for the call He placed on my life. I met my future wife, Missy, in high school. Her family noticed I was still bouncing from house to house and took me in, under strict guidelines. Her father, Steve, a strong Christian with a passion for the Lord and to witness to others, taught me the drywall business and, more importantly, how to walk with the Lord and be a Christian businessman full of integrity.

In 1994, I moved with them to Florida and worked in the family drywall business. Steve was known to be a hard worker, and he put me through the paces. This included a stretch of nine months working from sun up to sun down in hot South Florida without a day off.

I suspect it was an extreme test for me. He was trying to drive me off. Or, at least, he was testing the sincerity of my love for his daughter.

Missy and I married in 1996 and moved back to Fort Worth, and, in 1998, purchased a carpet cleaning franchise. We were the youngest owners for this particular brand in the United States. We began making money—a *lot* of money for a young couple.

And we spent a great deal of what we made because we weren't ready for success. At twenty-three-years-old, I wasn't mature enough to handle money very wisely. If we wanted something, we simply bought it without considering the consequences.

We began to ease away from going to church as our hearts were pulled away from God by the money and what it could get us. When difficult times hit, we weren't prepared, and the difficult times grew worse.

God has interesting ways of getting our attention. One spring, our church held a twelve-week Bible study on finances. I asked myself, *"What could the church possibly teach about business and money management out of the Bible?"*

I thought it was a joke or a trick to get me to give more money.

I was wrong. The class by Howard Dayton and Crown Ministries quickly opened my eyes, and I saw, for the first time, the wisdom of the Bible in the area of finance.

That small group study brought us to the intersection of faith and finances. We will all come to this intersection at some time in our lives. How we negotiate it will go a long way to determining our success in our walk with God and in life.

For me, I realized, I didn't have a financial problem. I had a spiritual problem that blocked me from living in all God had for me.

Growing up in an environment where our family didn't have much, yet surrounded by affluent kids, I had vowed to make a lot of money and to be successful. I was determined to achieve success and significance on my own. And now, years later, even as I was achieving those goals, I was hurting.

> I didn't have a financial problem. I had a spiritual problem that blocked me from living in all God had for me.

I surrendered to the Lord and prayed, "Lord, I've had enough. I'm tired of fighting this. I'm tired of this unhealthiness in my life, and I'll do whatever You call me to do."

And the Lord said, "Sell your business."

I was shocked, and I didn't want to sell the business. Yet, the Lord showed me it had become an idol. So we obeyed, and it sold within three weeks.

At the same time, Missy and I made the decision to live and run our business by faith. Right after we had our first child, a daughter we named Faith to match our decision, we moved back to Florida. We started a construction business under God's clear instruction to do it without any debt and to apply Biblical principles to everything we did. We started to get out of the debt we'd brought with us from Fort Worth. We were eking by, month-to-month, customer-to-customer, and God provided. Sometimes, it seemed like it was at the last second, but He always provided. Because of our obedience and God's faithfulness, the small drywall company grew, and we paid off $88,000 of personal debt as we built the business debt-free.

The calling I received at seventeen was renewed. I had run from that calling and focused on achieving success *my* way. When I gave myself back to the Lord, I knew I was called to be a pastor teaching on money, specifically in Southlake, Texas, which didn't make sense at the time since Southlake was just a rural community. But God knew what He had planned for that area, and what He told me came to pass many years later. After meeting Him at the intersection of faith and finances, I accepted His call. And, in His excellent timing, the door opened.

After a few years of diligent study of Larry Burkett books, listening to Dave Ramsey on the radio and Crown Ministry training, I started on my dream of teaching stewardship classes in whatever church would have me. This brought me into more contact with Crown Ministries. I called one day and told them I needed a box of brochures because I was going to start a stewardship ministry in every church in south Florida. Their Florida state representative, Tommy Beck, quickly contacted me and took me under his wing, training and mentoring me. He reined in my passions and exuberance and showed me how to focus them in order to bring greater glory to God and more good to His people. I was trained to be a financial counselor, small group leader and eventually served on staff at Crown Ministries as Southwest

Florida's local director for the Naples to Sarasota area (while self-funded by my drywall company).

God continued to prepare Missy and I for full-time ministry. I plugged into the Word with my usual *all-in* enthusiasm. I wanted to know every chapter in the Bible and every verse. My work was such that I could listen to an audio Bible and Bible commentaries. I was putting in so many hours, I frequently listened to the entire Bible in a week! I listened to Calvary Chapel expositional commentaries to get deeper into God's Word. One of my favorite teachers was Chuck Missler with Koinonia House ministry. I had every book of the Bible taught one hour per chapter from his ministry. Headphones on the job, keeping my mind and spirit plugged into the Word, I would log more than seventy hours per week.

The Lord prepared us to minister beyond the area of finances. We taught young married classes at church and watched the groups grow until we had to split them into smaller groups. We were learning how to minister to different kinds of people, developing our skills to be more effective for Him.

The next surprising step in my calling came when the church I grew up in back in Texas, The Hills Church, called and asked me to come and be their full-time stewardship minister. We agreed and, once again, God used my position to train and prepare me to develop my ministry gifts in new areas. I learned how to lead volunteers and how to train and prepare them to serve people. After completing a ministry development plan under the supervision of their experienced ministry staff, I was ordained to be a pastor.

One day in prayer, God told me to get ready to leave The Hills Church. I didn't want to; I was home and I loved my church family. I envisioned us staying at the church until Jesus came, serving and carrying out my mission—so did the church leadership. Missy and I prayed through it and were reluctantly ready to go whenever He gave the word.

A few months later, I received a call from Gateway Church, which was located 20 miles away in Southlake, Texas. They asked me to visit and help them start a stewardship ministry for their church. We began to meet, and I showed them how to build a comprehensive stewardship ministry. I gave them material and worked with them to develop a plan.

Two months later, they called back. They liked the plan, but after prayer, they wanted me to come on staff and lead a full stewardship department. I was not expecting this and wasn't sure I wanted to do it. The decision was one of the hardest I've ever had to make. When we both knew God was calling me to Gateway, we stepped out in obedience. Due to godly leadership at both churches, the transition went smoothly.

At Gateway, with the help of the full pastoral staff, we have built a growing and comprehensive stewardship ministry. The ministry seeks to serve four groups of people in the area of finances:

The Struggling,

The Stable,

The Solid,

The Surplused.

God's Word equips us to be wise stewards through helping us get out of debt and changing our lifestyles. When we make bad decisions, it's usually because of a lack of God's counsel. I've found that my bad decisions were ones I wasn't willing to share with others and seek their counsel. The keys I've found, and that I will share in this book, include knowing where your money is coming from and where it's going

> God's Word equips us to be wise stewards through helping us get out of debt and changing our lifestyles.

and making decisions based on a plan and wise counsel.

Several years ago, I was called into a meeting over lunch with our Senior Pastor, Robert Morris, and two other members of the senior pastoral staff. Pastor Robert told me he was releasing me to build a national and international stewardship ministry.

I thought I was being fired.

He didn't fire me—he commissioned me to be a stewardship evangelist. With Gateway as my platform, we have taken these generosity and stewardship principles to churches across the United States, to Israel and to Europe as the Lord has opened more doors for this message to spread through classes, teaching and now this book.

Needless to say, I didn't tithe my way into bankruptcy. Instead, I have been on an incredible adventure with Jesus as I have learned the Biblical principles to managing our finances.

In this book, I will share these Biblical principles and practical ways to apply them, so you can also walk in all the blessings God has for you. Let the adventure begin!

CHAPTER TWO

LIVING A BLESSED LIFE

THE BLESSED LIFE

The life message of my Senior Pastor, Robert Morris, is "The Blessed Life." This message has changed my life and the lives of thousands of others.

What is the blessed life you ask? Good question.

First, let me tell you what it is not. It is not a strategy to get rich. It is not a strategy for an easy or challenge-free life. It is not a health and wealth gospel. Any income level can live the blessed life.

The blessed life is all about the crazy adventure God has for each of us. Pastor Robert describes The blessed life as a life of supernatural powers working for you. The days of a blessed person are filled with divine "coincidences" and heavenly meaning.

Finances are part of it, but it's about more than finances. Money is simply a tool in the Christian's toolbox for living a blessed life. There are three primary elements to reaching and living the blessed life:

Lordship
Stewardship or Management
A Life of Generosity

LORDSHIP

Lordship is the cornerstone of living the blessed life. We are to honor God *with* everything and *in* everything. He calls for us to live generously and strategically. This makes room for Him to pour blessings into our lives. He is waiting for us to surrender so He can get us to the blessed life He has planned for us. We all have been created by God, who loves us, for a mission in this life. Walking in surrender to the Lordship of our Savior Jesus Christ is the only way to begin the blessed life journey.

The blessed life is not a prosperity theology—it is the reality of what Scripture says about being active in God's Kingdom. Prosperity theology is all about following God to get something for ourselves. It is a greedy, give-to-get philosophy. This is not what I teach. I teach a give-to-give and live-for-Christ's-advancement philosophy.

In the Word, Jesus has given us everything we need to live a blessed life, to live out everything He asks us to do. To make it work takes application, not just intellectual consent. When we apply His Word to our lives, we build them on the solid foundation of Jesus Himself.

As we dive into this study, be prepared to hear the Lord and to do what He says.

STEWARDSHIP

From the beginning, God created us and placed us to be stewards. In Genesis, we are commanded to have dominion over the world, to replenish the earth and to take care of it. We will get into this deeper in the next chapter.

Stewardship simply means management—management of the earth God created, and management of our time, talents, influence and resources.

The amount of money or time isn't what matters. What matters is what's in our hearts and what we are letting God do in our lives. God is looking for faithful stewards, people who will faithfully and wisely steward—or manage—time, talent and money. I believe He is preparing some to manage millions, billions and even trillions of dollars for His Kingdom.

A LIFE OF GENEROSITY

God does not leave us wondering how to do all this. Scripture is timeless and written for all generations. He is not surprised by life as we experience it in this modern age!

1 Timothy 6:17–19 is one of my favorite foundational stewardship passages. It's the verses God used to call me into ministry and the verses He takes me to when I ask Him lifestyle questions.

The Apostle Paul wrote to Timothy, who was a young pastor of the church of Ephesus, a growing church in a major seaport and economic center of the day. For us, the equivalent would be Boston, Houston or Los Angeles. Paul gave Timothy a short lesson on what to teach people who have resources.

> **1 Timothy 6:17–19**
> *Command those who are rich in this present world not to be arrogant nor to put their hope in wealth, which is so uncertain, but to put their hope in God, who richly provides us with everything for our enjoyment. Command them to do good, to be rich in good deeds, and to be generous and willing to share. In this way they will lay up treasure for themselves as a firm foundation for the coming age, so they may take hold of the life that is truly life.*

This passage tells us rich people's hope should be in God, not money. That's a good word for rich people, right? By the way, do you consider yourself rich? You might be surprised that, according to *globalrichlist.com*, if you make more than $47,000 per year, you are in the top 1.14% of the world. This means 98.86% of the world is behind you in available income!

So, in that sense, almost all of us are rich.

The reality of life is we can never have enough money to be secure, satisfied or feel significant. These needs are spiritual and are only met through our walk with God.

The blessed life does not rise or fall on our level of wealth, but within our walk with God. I used to think the car I drive and where I live give me personal value. Most of our culture has bought into this lie. The dangers of materialism are tremendous.

But don't misunderstand. There isn't anything wrong with having wealth. It simply needs to be managed and carefully stewarded. As you live the blessed life, chances are high you will have more money to steward. After all, the principle of sowing and reaping is a Biblical truth.

As we saw in 1 Timothy 6:17–19, God gives us stuff to enjoy. Let's not feel guilty about it. Watch for opportunities He brings our way to be generous. Let's embrace the responsibility God has given us to make a difference in this world. Part of the responsibility with God's resources is to live within our margins so we can be generous.

How much of a margin? There is no magic number or percentage. Life would be easier if God actually gave us the specific number, but He didn't. We all have to hear His voice for our specific calling. Through the material in this study, I hope to help you learn to hear His voice, then determine the best margin for you.

> Part of the responsibility with God's resources is to live within our margins so we can be generous.

Finally, these verses tell us we have a short opportunity

to make eternal investments. Have you noticed, life is short—and moving fast! *Carpe diem*—seize the day. We need to make the most of every opportunity to learn, to grow, to develop.

Jesus taught generosity results in treasure in heaven. We will touch on this in more detail in upcoming chapters, but, right now, pause and consider this thought: *"Do you live a life of supernatural powers working for you where your days are filled with divine 'coincidences' and heavenly meaning? If not, why not? Don't you want to?"*

I do, and it is an awesome adventure. From one steward to a fellow steward, come join me in the next chapter, and I will show you how to get to where you are living the blessed life.

CHAPTER THREE

STEWARD TO STEWARD

FIVE STEWARDSHIP PRINCIPLES

From my experience in counseling thousands of people and training hundreds of churches, I've discovered five principles everyone needs to understand. If you and I had the opportunity to sit down for a cup of coffee and I had just 30 minutes to talk to you about the most important observations on Biblical stewardship, from one steward to another, I would share five observations.

Observation #1

We are all created to be stewards.

Who are we? Our life identity is the most important, most impactful discovery of our life. To locate our identity, we have to go back to the beginning. There is a principle in Bible study called the Law of First Mention. What it means is wherever a subject or topic is first mentioned, it holds a higher or greater weight. Our identity as stewards shows up in the first chapter of Genesis, so it must be pretty important to God.

Genesis 1:1
In the beginning, God created the heavens and the earth.

Genesis 1:26 (NKJV)
Then God said, "Let Us make man in Our image, according to Our likeness; let them have dominion over the fish of the sea, over the birds of the air, and over the cattle, over all the earth and over every creeping thing that creeps on the earth."

That would include the bugs that creep in my garage.

God created us. Do not let that slip by. God created all of us and He created us to be stewards. Our job is to do the best we can as God's managers in whatever He sets before us. When I first understood this truth, it changed the way I thought of everything. Stewardship is a life-changing truth.

Stewardship has kind of lost its meaning and significance over the last few years, and I want to take it back to its powerful Biblical beginnings. Stewardship is not a fund-raising campaign. It's not just about money, and it's not about giving.

Stewardship is what happens with everything within us and around us. I am a steward of my family, my church, my house and cars, the money entrusted to me, my friendship and influence just to name a few.

When that Biblical revelation sinks in, it changes the way we view everything. One time I bought a two-year-old, brand new looking, fully loaded SUV. After dinner, as we walked out to the car, I noticed someone

> Stewardship is what happens with everything within us and around us.

had keyed the side of our truck. I was really mad! However, the edge of the anger wore off as I began to process this with the Lord. I asked why this had happened. I worked really hard in order to buy that truck. God said to me, "*I gave you the ability to buy that truck, and it really is Mine; you only manage it.*"

Honestly, this took some time to sink in, but I never fixed the truck because it served as a constant reminder to not get too attached to something as an owner, but to hold it loosely as a manager.

Observation #2
We have a mission, but it's broken.
God created everything. Then He created us with a purpose in our hearts—to take care of His creation (Genesis 1:26).

This mission was broken and destroyed by sin (Genesis 3). Ever since sin entered the world through Adam, we have been searching for success, significance and meaning in this life.

Paul says it this way:

Ephesians 2:10 (NKJV)
For we are His workmanship, created in Christ Jesus for good works, which God prepared beforehand that we should walk in them.

This was lost to us in Adam's sin.

Sin is an immoral act or transgression against God's divine law and we have all sinned. All sin requires a payment before a Holy God. Jesus is the promised payment of sin as God in the flesh Who came to earth living a sinless life and fulfilling thousands of years of extremely specific prophecy. Jesus paid for our sin, and by accepting His payment for our sin through faith, we can be made whole before God. All sin requires a perfect payment and no matter how good we are, we do not have the ability to live sinless lives or fulfill a payment for our sins. Jesus not only paid for our sin, He is the only key to fullness in life. Why do I cover this in a book on finances? Because many are looking for something only Christ can bring. But they use money and stuff to try to fill this void. This void can never be filled by possessions because they are not designed to satisfy us.

Sin destroys our ability to enjoy the gifts God gives us. It marks us with insecurity, anxiety and hopelessness. It creates the desire for us to get rich and build our own kingdom.

Matthew 6:24 (NKJV)
"No one can serve two masters; for either he will hate the one and love the other, or else he will be loyal to the one and despise the other."

We can't serve God and money.

Until we decide we're going to follow God at all costs, we won't reach our point of contentment. 1 Timothy 6:6 says, *"But Godliness with contentment is great gain."*

When we are secure in our salvation (and many Christians aren't), we can relax and not chase after stuff. The materialism breaks off, and God can begin to bless us as He measures our ability to be faithful in the small things before giving us the true riches of souls to manage.

It is a transformation of our hearts. Our understanding of the broken mission—of our sin—changes everything.

I'm spending time on this because I'm a pastor, and I love you. I want you to fully understand what salvation means. I don't want to spend eternity looking across the gulf at people in hell who sat under my teaching never understanding Christ's payment for their sin.

When you wrestle with the question: "Am I saved?" and come to a full understanding of what it means, it will be a lot easier to be a good steward because there's no resistance anymore.

Matthew 13:22 is our challenge.

> **Matthew 13:22** (NKJV)
> *"Now he who received seed among the thorns is he who hears the word, and the cares of this world and the deceitfulness of riches choke the word, and he becomes unfruitful."*

We can easily fall into this third seed realm—among the thorns. One of my goals is to make sure you aren't third-seed Christians.

Observation #3
Jesus is our Reconciler.

If you recognize your sin through breaking one of the moral laws of God, then you need a payment for that debt that you cannot pay. Have you ever lied, been angry, looked lustfully at someone not your spouse or even created an idea of who God is that is not accurate from Scripture? If you answered yes to any of these, then you have a need for Jesus. All it takes is one sin to spend eternity in hell. But I have great news. Jesus has reconciled all these things for us! His sacrifice brought us back into right relationship with our Father God. He is:

The foretold Messiah of Israel
Our Redeemer
The Designer and Orchestrator of our gifts
Creator of heaven and earth
Our Intercessor before God
Designer of our heavenly destiny
The Coming Ruler who will judge the world

Christ redeemed us from the curse of the law, and on the Day of

Judgment, our case will be dismissed due to a lack of evidence if we have accepted Him as our personal payment of sin.

By the way, did you know there are two ways to get to heaven? Okay, right now your heresy meters should be going off and your mind is saying, "What is he talking about?"

The first way is to never have a bad thought, never tell a lie, never be angry or lose your temper, never sin your whole life. Then, when you get to heaven, you can go to the throne room and tell Jesus, "Hey, move over. There's two of us now."

The second way is the path we are all on, which is to accept His payment for our sin and rely on what He did, not on what we can do.

If you have the need to accept the payment of your sin through Jesus' death on the cross, then repent and turn to Jesus. You can do this by praying this simple prayer between you and God. "Father, I am a sinner, and I need Your forgiveness for my sins. Please forgive me as I accept the payment Jesus Christ made for my sin. I accept Him as my Lord and Savior."

Yes, it really is that easy. God has made it that simple because of His love for you!

Now read John 3:16–17.

> "For God so loved the world that he gave his one and only Son, that whoever believes in him shall not perish but have eternal life. For God did not send his Son into the world to condemn the world, but to save the world through him."

Even if you are a Christian already, this should bring a big smile to your face! Now that you are saved, let's get to the mission ahead of us in life. What is next? Good question.

Where are we on this timeline of life, on this stretch of eternity? Let's look at Luke 19:11.

Luke 19:11

While they were listening to this, he went on to tell them a parable, because he was near Jerusalem and the people thought that the kingdom of God was going to appear at once.

This passage takes place as Jesus approaches Jerusalem on Palm Sunday. There's a huge crowd and a festive atmosphere. Many of Jesus' disciples and followers expected Him to waltz in, overthrow the Roman government and set up His own kingdom. In fact, some were arguing over who was going to be the greatest in the new kingdom and who would get to sit at His right hand.

They didn't quite understand what was going on and what Jesus was doing. He tells them this story, hoping they will catch it.

Let's continue with verses 12 through 14.

Luke 19:12–14

He said, "A man of noble birth went to a distant country to have himself appointed king and then to return. So he called ten of his servants and gave them ten minas. 'Put this money to work,' he said, 'until I come back.' But his subjects hated him and sent a delegation after him to say, 'We don't want this man to be our king.'"

If you look at this section of Scripture, you can divide the whole world into four groups. The first group is right here: those who reject Jesus.

Here's the second group:

Luke 19:15–17

"He was made king, however, and returned home. Then he sent for the servants to whom he had given the money, in order to find out what they had gained with it. The first one came and said, 'Sir,

your mina has earned ten more.' 'Well done, my good servant!'
his master replied. 'Because you have been trustworthy in a very
small matter, take charge of ten cities.'"

The third group is found in verses 18–19:

Luke 19:18–19

"The second came and said, 'Sir, your mina has earned five more.'
His master answered, 'You take charge of five cities.'"

Here's the fourth group:

Luke 19:20–27

"Then another servant came and said, 'Sir, here is your mina.
I have kept it laid away in a piece of cloth. I was afraid of you,
because you are a hard man. You take out what you did not put
in and reap what you did not sow.' His master replied, 'I will
judge you by your own words, you wicked servant! You knew, did
you, that I am a hard man, taking out what I did not put in, and
reaping what I did not sow? Why then didn't you put my money
on deposit, so that when I came back, I could have collected it
with interest?' Then he said to those standing by, 'Take his mina
away from him and give it to the one who has ten minas.' 'Sir,' they
said, 'he already has ten!' He replied, 'I tell you that to everyone
who has, more will be given, but as for the one who has nothing,
even what they have will be taken away. But those enemies of
mine who did not want me to be king over them—bring them
here and kill them in front of me.'"

This is a harsh, maybe even scary, passage. But it's the reality of
where we're living today.

We serve a King who's gone off to a foreign land to claim a country, and He'll be back someday. We're in that gap, in that time frame of waiting for His return. We have the opportunity for a ten-fold return or a five-fold return.

Or we can just give back what He's given us. "Hi Lord, I'm here. I made it. Don't have a lot to show for it, but I made it."

Observation #4
God's Word equips us to be stewards.
The Bible is the best book you can study on finances. There are over 2,000 passages on money, and seventeen of the thirty-eight parables Jesus taught are about money. To not have an understanding of God's Word on money is a significant disadvantage in our walk with Christ. It's a significant disadvantage in life!

You can pick up any non-Christian book on finances and find a Biblical root or foundation that is the genesis for the author's ideas and concepts.

Any asset left unmanaged becomes a liability. It's critical we not only understand the theology about money, but also the practical application. My goal as we walk through this book is to equip you to manage money

> The Bible is the best book you can study on finances.

so you can take the principles from God's Word and apply them to your finances.

Recently, I was teaching on this in Israel. I was having a good time sharing these principles, but the Israeli people are a little different. They push back at what you're saying and challenge a lot. It's part of their culture. I enjoyed the challenge immensely.

One gentleman said to me, "These are Western culture ideas that won't work here in Israel."

My answer was, "These verses were written to Israelis in the land you live in today over the last several thousand years. These are not Western principles. They were written to your people in your land in a much worse and more oppressed time period than you live in today. All it's going to take—just like it did when they were first written—is for you to step out and walk by faith. These are Biblical ideas that are timeless and have no region."

It was like a cloud lifted out of the room as he grasped the concept that God's Word prepares us to be stewards.

Observation #5
We have one life to make an eternal difference.
According to the 2007 U.S. Census Bureau on World Vital Events, there is a death every 1.8 seconds, 105 per minute, 6,306 every hour, 151,338 every day, 4,603,198 every month and 55,238,376 every year![1] Not a happy thought.

And I can guarantee you one thing—just about all of them were surprised when it actually happened. I see this when I do hospital visits and counsel terminally ill people. No matter how much preparation they had, it is still a surprise.

Death is like a period in the middle of a sentence.

God wired us for eternity. We naturally think we will live forever. Unfortunately, our broken mission creates the brevity of life, but we don't think about it in those terms. I'm not trying to scare anyone, but I do want you to grasp the weight of this so we can get on with living our calling.

There are several ways to miss our calling. One is to run the wrong race, build the wrong kingdom, pour ourselves into our own self-existence or into something that doesn't matter.

Another is to get so wrapped up in greed where we never have

---

[1] *census.gov/cgi-bin/ipc/pcwe*

enough and our focus is always on getting more.

Third, we fall into analysis paralysis. We never quite figure out what God is calling us to because we question and analyze. We look for another sign and then another, and we end up not moving at all. God can only guide a moving ship. If you've ever ridden a jet ski, did you notice that until you hit the gas, it wouldn't steer?

But the most critical way to miss our calling is to not accept Christ as our Lord and Savior.

My first service as a volunteer in church ministry was watching babies in children's ministry. I moved on to making announcements at the beginning of Sunday school class. Then I was tricked, due to my terror of public speaking, into teaching half of the Sunday school lesson in the young marrieds class. The next thing I know, I'm teaching the entire hour-long lesson, and at the time, I was still terrified about speaking in front of people.

> The most critical way to miss our calling is to not accept Christ as our Lord ad Savior.

God used that to build my confidence, and now I'm leading a church stewardship movement all over the country as well as in Europe and Israel.

Each step in this journey was terrifying, yet each step solidified my heart because God had given me a word, and each step pushed me forward to the fulfillment of His word.

To achieve your calling, you will need to determine your gifts. In Chapter 8, we'll talk about life stewardship and you'll learn how to find your gift set. You'll analyze your gifts to really determine what God created you for. We'll walk through a process to figure out how to move in that direction using your life to make a difference.

Part of achieving your calling is to focus on your strengths, not your weaknesses. Weaknesses are hard to improve. We will be more successful when we build on our strengths and on the giftings God has given us. The opportunity to make an eternal difference only happens once. Let's get aggressive preparing our life for maximum return on investment.

PRACTICAL APPLICATIONS

Route 7 Road Map

The Generous Life Route 7 road map is a tool to help you apply Biblical principles in a simple and systematic way to your finances. The map has seven steps with clear sub-steps to complete on the journey. Notice in the seven steps there are giving, spending and saving elements as well as verse locations to help anchor the financial principles to the Bible.

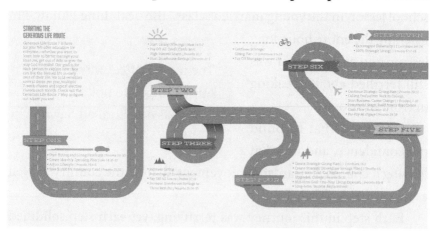

Step One

- **Start tithing and giving firstfruit offerings.**
  Proverbs 3:9–10 (NKJV)
  Honor the Lord with your possessions, and with the firstfruits of all your increase; so your barns will be filled with plenty, and your vats will overflow with new wine.

■ **Create a monthly spending plan.**
  Luke 14:28–30
  "Suppose one of you wants to build a tower. Won't you first sit down and estimate the cost to see if you have enough money to complete it? For if you lay the foundation and are not able to finish it, everyone who sees it will ridicule you, saying, 'This person began to build and wasn't able to finish.'"

■ **Adjust your lifestyle.**
  Proverbs 23:4–5
  Do not wear yourself out to get rich; do not trust your own cleverness. Cast but a glance at riches, and they are gone, for they will surely sprout wings and fly off to the sky like an eagle.

This gives us the margin I wrote about earlier to begin to go where God wants us to go financially.

■ **Save $1,000 for an emergency fund.**
  Proverbs 21:20 (NASB)
  There is precious treasure and oil in the dwelling of the wise, but a foolish man swallows it up.

CHAPTER FOUR

FIRST THINGS FIRST

GIVING

I can picture you wincing and groaning. Most people do when they hear anything about tithing, giving or generosity because they've been wounded in this area. As I said earlier, there's been a lot of wrong teaching about giving.

God's heart is not to make you feel guilty or put you under condemnation. I promise never to point my finger and yell at you about giving. Romans 8:1 tells us *"there is no condemnation for those who are in Christ Jesus."*

Using guilt and condemnation to get people to give is simply not fair. It robs the joy of the whole experience. So let's get rid of all condemnation in the area of giving, whether it's from people in the church or from self-condemnation. Condemnation is the hammer of the Enemy—his tool to beat us down and take us further from God.

In my teaching and counseling, I've observed most people are like a piñata when it comes to giving. They're not balanced—they swing from one side to the other. They're either completely for it or completely against it. They don't really have any balance in their lives in this area.

This is all part of the Enemy's game. If he can stop people from tithing and giving, no matter by what means, they'll miss out on a lot of the blessings in their lives, and the Enemy will strive to have them blame God for it.

If people do become generous in their giving, then the Enemy says, "Yeah, but look at all you keep." People with a generous heart give to serve the Lord, then feel guilty because they're not doing enough.

Everyone who is generous struggles with this.

THE ROOT OF GENEROSITY

Biblical generosity is rooted in love.

God set the example all through the Bible. It culminates in John 3:16.

John 3:16
"For God so loved the world that he gave his one and only Son, that whoever believes in him shall not perish but have eternal life."

In Romans 5:8, we learn, *"God demonstrates his own love for us in this: While we were still sinners, Christ died for us."*

Because of His love, He willingly died for us.

The early church followed this example:

2 Corinthians 8:1–4
And now, brothers, we want you to know about the grace that God has given the Macedonian churches. Out of the most severe trial, their overflowing joy and their extreme

*poverty welled up in rich generosity. For I testify that they
gave as much as they were able, and even beyond their ability.
Entirely on their own, they urgently pleaded with us for the
privilege of sharing in this service to the saints.*

Severe trial, overwhelming joy, extreme poverty. And they gave.

At its core, generosity is a heart issue.

Before they entered the Promised Land, Moses gave the Israelites
a lesson on their hearts (Deuteronomy 15:4–18).

Deuteronomy 15:4–6 *(emphasis added)*
*However, there should be no poor among you, for in the
land the Lord your God is giving you to possess as your
inheritance, he will richly bless you, if only you fully obey the
Lord your God and are careful to follow all these commands
I am giving you today. For the Lord your God will bless you
as he promised, and you will lend to many nations but will
borrow from none. You will rule over many nations but
none will rule over you.*

There are four phases of the heart identified in this passage. Everyone
who goes on a generosity journey falls into these four categories at
some point in time.

Deuteronomy 15:7–9 *(emphasis added)*
*If there is a poor man among your brothers in any of the
towns of the land that the Lord your God is giving you, do
not be **greedy or tightfisted** toward your poor brother. Rather
be openhanded and freely lend him whatever he needs. Be
careful not to harbor this wicked thought: "The seventh
year, the year of reconciling debts, is near," so that you do*

not show ill will toward your needy brother and give him nothing. He may then appeal to the Lord against you, and you will be found guilty of sin.

The selfish or tightfisted heart was me early in my walk with the Lord when I first heard teachings on giving. I thought I was generous, but I wasn't. I was focused on myself and any giving I did was done reluctantly. I wasn't concerned with where the gift was going or what it accomplished. It was all about me.

Deuteronomy 15:10–11 *(emphasis added)*
*Give generously to him and do so without a **grudging heart**; then because of this the Lord your God will bless you in all your work and in everything you put your hand to. There will always be poor in the land. Therefore I command you to be openhanded toward your brothers and toward the poor and needy in your land.*

The grudging or grieving heart says, "I'll try it, but I'll be grieved about it." There is a level of resentment about giving. We give out of coerced obedience, not our heart. In this category, we forget that when we cheerfully obey, God can do something great.

Deuteronomy 15:12–14 *(emphasis added)*
*If a fellow Hebrew, a man or a woman, sells himself to you and serves you six years, in the seventh year you must let him go free. And when you release him, do not send him away empty-handed. Supply him **generously** from your flock, your threshing floor and your winepress. Give to him as the Lord your God has blessed you.*

The generous heart enjoys giving. Matthew 6:21 reminds us, *"for where your treasure is, there your heart will be also."*

Deuteronomy 15:15 *(emphasis added)*
*Remember that you were slaves in Egypt and **the Lord your God redeemed you (grateful heart)**. That is why I give you this command today.*

The grateful heart sees giving as the way to express our gratefulness for all God has done for us and given us.

All around me, I see the wrecked lives and messes created by people who haven't walked with Jesus, who haven't stepped into this blessed life. And, while I grieve for them and help them however I can, it makes me glad I'm a giver. When I think about what a mess my life was before Christ and how far the Lord has brought me, I settle into a grateful frame of mind.

The scripture says there will always be poor in the land. Why? Is it only because people don't handle money wisely and make poor decisions?

In my former church, I counseled a middle-aged man who was somewhat mentally challenged. He could work and pretty much take care of himself, but he couldn't handle his finances. He was constantly in financial crisis or on the brink of one. I negotiated with utility and credit card companies on his behalf, which kept him going until the next crisis hit. But our plans always imploded.

> The grateful heart sees giving as the way to express our gratefulness for all God has done for us and given us.

Once, he received a lump sum settlement of $80,000, yet was back soon to see me with another crisis. When I asked him what happened to the settlement, he told me he spent it on baseball cards.

I vented to my covering pastor about this—we pastors do this from time to time, you know—questioning why this man was in my life.

My pastor said, "You don't know?"

"No," I said. "And I wouldn't mind if he was out of my life."

"He's in your life for you."

This stopped me short because I thought he had gone crazy. Then he explained the poor in the land is a test of our heart. What are we going to do with them? How are we going to help them?

This is what really nailed me: What is our *attitude* as we do it?

Is our heart grateful, generous, grieving or selfish?

When people are habitually in a crisis cycle, it's not a financial issue. It's a spiritual problem. A poverty mentality—a weapon of the Enemy—has taken over.

It's the church's responsibility to take care of the poor—not the government's. The church not only needs to help with the immediate crisis, it must also mentor and teach the poor so they can be delivered from their bondage of poverty and walk fully in all God has for them.

> When people are habitually in a crisis cycle, it's not a financial issue. It's a spiritual problem.

God's heart is for the poor. Our job is to join Him in ministering to them. If your brother goes off in need, he will complain to the Lord, and it will be sin for you.

DEVELOPING A GENEROUS AND GRATEFUL HEART

How do we develop this generous and grateful heart?

By applying the "Principle of the First" to our income. This is not only a powerful standard to live by, it is also a test. A test we face every time we get paid.

Proverbs 3:4–5 tells us, *"Trust in the Lord with all your heart and lean not on your own understanding; in all your ways acknowledge him, and he will make your paths straight."*

All through the Scriptures, God gives us vivid object lessons of His ownership, our stewardship responsibilities and a foretold Jesus the Messiah. The whole Bible is an object lesson about Jesus. If you find something in the Scripture you don't understand, just think *"It's about Jesus,"* and that will help you figure it out.

Even the Principle of the First is about Jesus. Follow along with me as we look at this in God's words.

> **Exodus 13:1–2** (NKJV)
> *Then the Lord spoke to Moses, saying, "Concentrate to Me all the firstborn, whatever opens the womb among the children of Israel, both of man and beast; it is Mine."*

> **Exodus 13:12–13** (NKJV)
> *"That you shall set apart to the Lord all that open the womb, that is, every firstborn that comes from an animal which you have; all the males shall be the Lord's. But every firstborn of a donkey you shall redeem with a lamb; and if you will not redeem it, then you shall break its neck. And all the firstborn of man among your sons you shall redeem."*

Every time one of their animals delivered its firstborn, they had to sacrifice it, or, if it was unclean, they had to redeem it with a lamb. In Hebrew culture, the donkey is considered unclean while the lamb is treasured.

The idea of sacrificing the firstborn is not as strong in our culture, so we tend not to see the significance of this. It doesn't impact us like it did the Hebrews.

God's portion was devoted, or consecrated, to Him at the Temple. He commands the firstborn be sacrificed or redeemed.

Do you realize what this means?

Jesus is the Lamb. He is God's firstborn Son, and He is clean. We are unclean. Therefore, just as it is described in Exodus, the clean (Jesus) was sacrificed so we (the unclean) could be redeemed.

The New Testament Church met on Sunday because of the Principle of the First. They gave the first day of the week to the Lord.

The premise of the Principle of the First is that firstfruits must be offered to God.

> **Exodus 23:19** (NKJV) *(emphasis added)*
> *"The first of the **firstfruits** of your land you shall bring into the house of the Lord your God."*

> **Proverbs 3:9–10** (NKJV) *(emphasis added)*
> *Honor the Lord with your possessions, and with the **firstfruits** of all your increase; so your barns will be filled with plenty, and your vats will overflow with new wine.*

Because God's portion is given to the temple, it has a blessing. If it's not given to God, the firstfruits are cursed because they are stolen.

Let's see how the Principle of the First applied in the example of Cain and Abel.

> **Genesis 4:3–5** (NKJV)
> *And in the process of time it came to pass that Cain brought an offering of the fruit of the ground to the Lord. Abel also brought of the firstborn of his flock and of their fat. And the Lord respected Abel and his offering. But He did not respect Cain and his offering.*

Why did God accept Abel's offering and not Cain's? Cain's was not a firstfruit. He violated the Principle of the First. *"In the process of time,"* Cain brought the fruit of the ground, not the firstfruit—just what he felt like bringing at the time.

Abel, on the other hand, did follow the Principle of the First. He brought the firstborn of his flock. And God honored him because he honored God.

THE TITHE MUST BE BROUGHT FIRST

I can hear the Dragnet theme rolling around in your mind. But bear with me, and I think you'll see how important this ordinance is to God and how it can affect not only your finances, but your relationship with Him as well.

An ordinance simply means a decree of ordinary behavior. God wants tithing to be as natural to us as breathing.

The tithe is ten percent of our income. It is an amount. Firstfruits is a position. Basically, this means we bring the first ten percent of our income to God.

In the Old Testament, during the time of King Hezekiah's reign, the temple had fallen into disarray and society had run amuck. In cleaning out the temple, they discovered the scrolls of the law and brought them to Hezekiah. He ordered they be read to the people and revival broke out as they heard the law and applied it to everything they ran across.

> God wants tithing to be as natural to us as breathing.

2 Chronicles 31:5 (NKJV) *(emphasis added)*
*As soon as the commandment was circulated, the children of Israel **brought** in abundance the **firstfruits** of grain and wine, oil and honey and of all the produce of the field; and they **brought** in abundantly the **tithe** of everything.*

They began to honor the Lord with their firsts and everything flourished around them.

The Church needs to rediscover the principle of the tithe. As they do, and as the Lord begins to bless them, they also need to rediscover the principles of stewardship and watch what God does in the society around them through their faithful generosity. I guarantee it will be transformational.

This is already evident in my church. Gateway Church is an extremely generous church full of stories of radical giving. Many surveys show Gateway as doubling, and even tripling, the giving of most churches. This is because the people have been taught the truth about tithing and learned to live God's way.

I'm looking forward to the next twenty years watching the impact on society as we plant churches and raise up congregations in these principles.

God instituted these principles because He knew it was both a filtering process and a strengthening process for our hearts. He knew it was a way to bless and create spiritual revival and fervency in a community.

Malachi 3:7–12 (NKJV)

"Yet from the days of your fathers you have gone away from My ordinances and have not kept them. Return to Me, and I will return to you," says the Lord of hosts. "But you said, 'In what way shall we return?' Will a man rob God? Yet you have robbed Me! But you say, 'In what way have we robbed You?' In tithes and offerings. You are cursed with a curse, for you have robbed Me, even this whole nation. Bring all the tithes into the storehouse, that there may be food in My house, and try me now in this," says the Lord of hosts, "If I will not open for you the windows of heaven and pour out

*for you such a blessing that there will not be room enough
to receive it. And I will rebuke the devourer for your sakes,
so that he will not destroy the fruit of your ground, nor shall
the vine fail to bear fruit for you in the field," says the Lord
of hosts. "And all the nations will call you blessed, for you
will be a delightful land," says the Lord of hosts.*

God is telling them they have gone away from His ordinances, His system of ordinary behavior. But if they return, they will be blessed. He even challenges them to test Him on this. Do it and see what happens.

*Note: The tithe is never given, it is always brought or returned.
God gives my income, my harvest, to me, and I return the first
ten percent to Him. How can I give something that is not mine?*

Suppose I lent my car to a friend and, when he was done, he decided to give me the car. He can't give me my own car. He can only return it to me.

And the tithe is not mine to designate. It's clear in Deuteronomy 12:5–17 and 14:22–29 it goes to the House of God.

SOME QUESTIONS AND OBJECTIONS ABOUT THE TITHE

When do you pay the tithe? Is it possible to give ten percent and not be tithing?

Let's say you get paid on Thursday. You pay all your bills and then buy groceries. Next, you write the tithe check before you come to church on Sunday.

Are we really giving in faith when we give ten percent *after* we've paid all our bills first? Aren't we revealing *our* priorities when we *willingly* pay everybody else first and then we see if there's enough left over to bring God His portion?

There are so many blessings that go along with tithing, but they only work under the ***principle of putting God first***. And the principle of faith initiates the blessings.

Isn't tithing part of the law; part of the Old Testament?

The principle of the tithe supersedes the law. Abel, the first tither, gave a tithe 2,500 years before the law.

For another example, look at what transpired between Abraham and Melchizedek:

> **Genesis 14:18–20** (NKJV)
> *Then Melchizedek king of Salem brought out bread and wine; he was the priest of God Most High. And he blessed him and said: "Blessed be Abram of God Most High, Possessor of heaven and earth; and blessed be God Most High, who has delivered your enemies into your hand." And he gave him a tithe of all.*

Abraham, our spiritual father, tithed to Melchizedek. This took place long before God gave the law to Moses.

Jacob tithed 400 years before the law:

> **Genesis 28:22** (NKJV)
> *"And this stone which I have set as a pillar shall be God's house, and of all that You give me I will surely give a tenth to You."*

Is murder part of the law? Yes. *"Thou shalt not kill."* Was murder okay prior to the law? No. You can't kill each other. Cain was punished for killing Abel.

Now that we no longer live under the law but we live under Grace, can we kill each other? No. It's still not right.

Does tithing apply to New Testament believers? Isn't it just Old Testament?

Jesus and Paul both affirm the tithe. Matthew's Gospel is in the New Testament, and the words are in red so we know Jesus spoke them.

> **Matthew 23:23** (NKJV) *(emphasis added)*
> *"Woe to you, scribes and Pharisees, hypocrites (and other miscellaneous jerks). For you pay tithe of mint and anise and cumin, and have neglected the weightier matters of the law: justice and mercy and faith. These you ought to have done, without leaving the others undone." (Also Luke 12:34)*

Jesus believes and teaches tithing is still part of what we're called to do.

In Hebrews 7:1–8, we learn Melchizedek is an Old Testament appearance of Jesus.

> **Hebrews 7:1–8** (NKJV)
> *For this Melchizedek, king of Salem, priest of the Most High God, who met Abraham returning from the slaughter of the kings and blessed him, to whom also Abraham gave a tenth part of all, first being translated "king of righteousness," and then also king of Salem, meaning "king of peace," without father, without mother, without genealogy, having neither beginning of days nor end of life, but made like the Son of God, remains a priest continually. Now consider how great this man was, to whom even the patriarch Abraham gave a tenth of the spoils. And indeed those who are the sons of Levi, who receive the priesthood, have a commandment to receive tithes from the people according to the law, that is, from their brethren, though they have come from the loins*

of Abraham; but he whose genealogy is not derived from them received tithes from Abraham and blessed him who had the promises. Now beyond all contradiction the lesser is blessed by the better. Here mortal men receive tithes, but there he receives them, of whom it is witnessed that he lives.

Today, mortal men receive and administer the tithe. This is a big deal that every pastor has to take seriously. We are a spiritual priesthood of the lineage of the Levites, administering the gifts of the people to further God's Kingdom. This is a heavy responsibility for the pastoral ministry, one they should take seriously.

Do we tithe on the gross or the net?

I believe and teach we should tithe on our gross income. If I'm wrong, I'd rather be on the side of generosity. Besides, who do you think will bless your money: the government or God?

Does the entire tithe go to the church?

Deuteronomy 12:11 (NKJV) *(emphasis added)*
"then there will be **the place where the Lord your God chooses to make His name abide.** *There you shall bring all that I command you; your burnt offerings, your sacrifices, your* **tithes,** *the heave offerings of your hand, and all your choice offerings which you vow to the Lord."*

Malachi 3:10 reminds us to *"Bring all the* **tithes to the storehouse."**
Acts 4:34–35 describes how there were no needy people among the early church because the congregation would bring money to the apostles to give to those in need.

It's clear the tithe goes to the church—the place God calls home.

Should I get out of debt first?

The third chapter of Proverbs tells us to trust in the Lord with all my heart, to honor my Lord with my firstfruits.

If I'm determined to get out of debt, I want God on my side. I want His blessings on my finances so I can get out of debt more quickly.

It's much better to work with the tailwind of His blessing than against a headwind of disobedience.

What if my spouse disagrees?

At one seminar, a couple sat on the front row, and I could tell he did not want to be there. He'd been dragged there against his will. I could tell from his posture he thought my teaching was a huge waste of his time. He sat with arms crossed, not taking notes, looking like he'd rather have a root canal—without anesthesia!

Next to him, his wife was leaning forward, writing down everything I said, giving him the occasional elbow when I made a point she really liked.

I get to the Q&A part, and she pops right up, the first question out of the box.

> It's much better to work with the tailwind of His blessing than against a headwind of disobedience.

"I want to tithe but my husband won't let me. Are my finances cursed? He doesn't want to give to the church. I want to know—do I follow God or do I follow my husband?"

His eyes were as big as saucers. Everyone held their breath. You could have heard a pin drop! I think he was too shocked to say anything. I'll tell you, I really wanted to be a fly on the wall on that drive home!

The Lord gave me the grace and wisdom to answer her. I explained the Lord had put a structure in our lives, in the family, in a marriage: the husband is the head of the household. If she and her husband were not in agreement on something, I told her it was her responsibility and obligation to serve and obey her husband.

Sometimes, as spouses, we have to duck and pray. We have to get out of the way so God can have a clear shot at our husband or wife. My advice is, if you're not in unity, and it's adding stress to your relationship, take a break. Step aside and pray about it and see where God leads.

These principles are not in place to drive a wedge between people. They were instituted to draw people closer to each other and to God.

Tithing is under the Old Testament and we're not under that anymore. The function of the law is to take us to Christ. Galatians 3:4 tells us: _"Therefore the law was our tutor to bring us to Christ, that we might be justified by faith."_

If I hadn't been challenged with tithing, I would not have grown in my relationship with Jesus. I don't think I'd be a pastor today. In fact, I'm sure I'd be a self-centered businessman, and I would not have grown.

The law did exactly what it was supposed to do in my life. It convicted me and drew me closer to Jesus.

> **Romans 15:4** (NKJV)
> _For whatever things were written before were written for our learning, that we through the patience and comfort of the Scriptures might have hope._

All things in the Word are written for our learning, growing and understanding. We can actually rip out that divider between the Old and New Testaments. All sixty-six books and forty different authors are all part of the same central message system, all pointing us to Jesus as the way to a blessed life here on earth and the eternal life to follow.

> **2 Timothy 3:16–17** (NKJV)
> *All Scripture is given by inspiration of God, and is profitable for doctrine, for reproof, for correction, for instruction in righteousness, that the man of God may be complete, thoroughly equipped for every good work.*

In my denomination growing up, we discounted the Old Testament when making theological decisions. We were taught the Old Testament, but we focused on Matthew through Revelation for guidance in our daily lives. We included Psalms and Proverbs because they were nice.

This actually was a disservice to me because I didn't fully understand the Spirit of the Lord. When it came to the New Testament, I thought God had changed His mind and given us a new set of rules.

It's really exciting when we discover how integrated the Scriptures really are. The New Testament is in the Old Testament concealed and the Old Testament is in the New Testament revealed.

Some people have told me: "I don't want to tithe."

Then don't. But you have a deeper issue than tithing. I'm not trying to talk you into tithing. I'm explaining the principles God has given us throughout His Word for living a life fully blessed. I can't force you into it. God wants us to give willingly and cheerfully.

If you don't want to tithe—don't tithe. It's your choice. If you want to live cursed, that's your prerogative.

Tithing and firstfruits are indicators of our heart and when we put God first, we are blessed. It's as simple as that.

Would you rather try to make it through life with one hundred percent and all of it cursed or with ninety percent and all of it redeemed and blessed?

THE LAW OF MULTIPLICATION

In some circles, the law of multiplication gets a bad rap. Prosperity gospel teachers have taught some scriptures in this accurately and some not so accurately.

The rub happens because in Scripture, God says if you do this, this and this, you will be blessed and this and that is going to happen. What gets lost is: why are we blessed?

We're blessed so we can create reciprocal relationships. God blesses us. We in turn bless others. It becomes a cycle through which everyone benefits.

The problem arises—and this is where the prosperity gospel goes wrong—when we become a reservoir instead of a conduit.

God blesses, and we raise our lifestyle.

God blesses, and we buy jewelry.

God blesses, and the next thing you know, I've got a Rolls Royce.

In this mentality, God is my genie, and I'm going to be abundantly rich. Maybe God *will* have you become rich, but that's not the motivation behind the principle. That's not why He instituted tithes and offerings. Giving to get isn't His plan. Giving to get is materialism.

Look at 2 Corinthians 9:6–11.

> **2 Corinthians 9:6–11** (emphasis added)
> *Remember this: Whoever sows sparingly will also reap sparingly, and whoever sows generously will also reap generously. Each man should give what he has decided in his heart to give, not reluctantly or under compulsion, for God loves a cheerful giver. And God is able to make **all** grace abound to you, so that in **all** things at **all** times, having **all***

*that you need, **you will abound in every good work**. As it is written: "He has scattered abroad his gifts to the poor; his righteousness endures forever." Now he who supplies seed to the sower and bread for food will also supply and increase your store of seed and will enlarge the harvest of your righteousness. You will be made rich in every way so that **you can be generous on every occasion**, and through us your generosity will result in thanksgiving to God.*

Count how many times the word "all" is used in this passage. They're amazing scriptures. Stick them on your dashboard or refrigerator. Aim for becoming generous. It is discussing two types of giving over and above the tithe: *offerings* and *extravagant offerings*. Offerings are what we give over our 10% tithe. Extravagant offerings are large percentage gifts that are sometimes hard to rationalize; however, they are very satisfying, rewarding and even sometimes scary to participate in, but when you know you've heard from God about what to give, it is always the right thing to do! Abraham being willing to offer Isaac was an extravagant offering. God offering Jesus on our behalf—now that is an exceptional extravagant offering!

God will expand your seed when you are looking to expand His Kingdom.

Remember Luke 19 and the parable of the talents? Which steward received the other steward's talent? The one who had already received the ten—the one who did the best with what he had, the one who multiplied the Master's resources.

If we don't get this right, it will become a hindrance in all areas of our finances, of our relationships and in all areas where God speaks

> God will expand your seed when you are looking to expand His Kingdom.

into our lives.

Sometimes I wonder if I'm getting this whole generosity thing right in my own family. Am I setting the right example? Am I having a positive impact?

And then God shows me something in my kids.

It was Christmas time, and we stopped at a Taco Bueno with the kids. There was an older woman working there, and we could see from her countenance and demeanor, something was not right. I asked her how she was doing.

She told us she was doing okay. She'd lost her husband a couple of years earlier and never had to work outside the home before. She was working now to earn some extra Christmas money. She was struggling and wanted to bless her kids for Christmas. I offered to pray for her, but she declined and wandered on.

Our ten-year-old daughter said she wanted to give the woman all her money. She had saved $100 to buy a special bird. We agreed with her decision. As we headed home to get her money, the six-year-old and thirteen-year-old said they wanted to give too.

I told my wife we needed to stop by the bank because I wanted to be part of this as well.

The kids really cleaned out everything for her. They included Bible bucks and gift cards they'd received along with cash.

We returned to the Taco Bueno and sent the kids in alone to give her the money. This was their idea, and we wanted them to experience the fullness of what they were doing. They ran in and said to the woman, "Jesus wants to bless you." They gave her the envelope and ran off. They didn't know what else to do.

As we drove around the restaurant to leave, we glanced in the window, and the woman was sobbing.

And I thought, *"Yeah, we're getting it right in this area for our kids."*

This is the heart the Father wants to see in His people.

PRACTICAL APPLICATIONS

Lifestyle Adjustments

Any time you do something like Route 7, it always calls for changes and raises questions. One is in the area of lifestyle adjustments. If you've started using a budgeting system, you've probably faced the question: "How do I get my budget to balance if it doesn't quite line up?" There are really only three things you can do if more money goes out than comes in.

1. Make More Money

This is what guys usually think of as the first response. Get a second job. Work more hours. This is actually not the most efficient response because you tend to lose thirty to thirty-five percent of the extra money. You pay more in taxes, plus there's additional wear-and-tear on your cars and your clothing, as well as other expenses. And think about how it affects your family and personal relationships.

2. Spend Less

This is the most efficient thing you can do. Look at where your money is going. You will find some place to cut spending. But if you can't spend less or if the lessened spending doesn't seem to be doing the job quickly enough, look at number three.

3. Sell Stuff

Take an inventory of your stuff. Is there something you haven't used in a while? Sell it, especially if it's a high-ticket item. Set a time limit. If you haven't used it in "x" amount of time, sell it. A caution: This is not always the most efficient way to balance your budget because it frequently is only a one-time thing. Also, you may need the item down the road, and it could be more expensive to replace.

Ultimately, your lifestyle decisions and desires determine the direction you will go in your life.

There are four groups of people in the world.

Group One

These are the ones who are on their calling (living the life God called them to live with genuine satisfaction) and in good shape financially. If you're in this group, the pressure and intensity of your lifestyle decisions are not as severe because you're on the mark, you're where you should be and steadily improving. In the Parable of the Sower, this is the group who is fertile soil and receiving thirty, sixty and hundredfold returns.

Group Two

These are on their calling but in bad shape financially. The intensity and pressure are greater for this group because of the increased financial pressure to make changes and the sense that you are setting a bad example in ministry, in your business or job and your family. In the Parable of the Sower, this is group who hears the Word, but the blessing is choked by the cares of this world.

Group Three

These are off their calling but in good shape financially. The people in this group probably feel more spiritual pressure because they're not sure yet what God's called them to do, and they may be in some fear about what His calling may mean financially. In the Parable of the Sower, this is the group who hears the Word but doesn't understand it, and it is snatched from their hearts.

> When I was in construction, we intentionally lived under our means because I knew I was called to be a pastor, but I wasn't in that season of life yet. I made a six-figure income, and I drove one hundred dollar cars—on purpose. I invested enough to get them started and drove them into the ground—which sometimes didn't take too long. I wanted to be in the position that when God said, "Now is the time to step into full-time ministry," I would be ready and able to do it without being concerned about how we would make it financially. When I entered the ministry, I took a one hundred thousand dollar pay cut. We were able to do it because the lifestyle decisions we made put us in good shape with our finances and our spirits.

Group Four

These are the ones who are off their calling and are in bad shape financially. This group is a recipe for pure frustration and disaster, and they are probably feeling intense pressure. Their lifestyle decisions are based on immediate and urgent needs—pay the rent, buy food, keep the electricity on. They are in survival mode and not living the desires of their heart. In the Parable of the Sower, this is the first group who hears the Word, but it never takes root.

As you begin to budget and pull your finances together, keep these four groups in mind as you work through the process. Pray for God's wisdom for you to move into Group One. It will help you determine the answers to these questions:

How much do I keep?

How much do I cut?

How radical do I want to go?

Some Final Thoughts on Lifestyle

The lifestyle we choose should be lived with joy. Enjoy your lifestyle. If you're not enjoying it, figure out what needs to change.

The Bible does not define a Christian lifestyle; I wish it did. However, God did use all types of people to illustrate and establish His principles. He used the poor, the wealthy, the sick, the healthy, the maimed, the politicians, the soldiers and the religious leaders.

Our culture encourages us to spend all that we make and even more (thus we have credit cards). It teaches us to be discontented because it attaches our self-worth to our net worth. These are all lies.

Paul sums it up beautifully in Philippians 4:11–13.

> **Philippians 4:11–13** (NASB)
> *I have learned to be content in whatever circumstances I am. I know how to get along with humble means, and I also know how to live in prosperity; in any and every circumstance I have learned the secret of being filled and going hungry, both of abundance and suffering need. I can do all things through Him who strengthens me.*

When we put Christ as the central focal point of our lives, we can do all He calls us to do.

CHAPTER FIVE

THE SPENDING PLAN

Several years ago, "Saturday Night Live" did a skit about budgeting. It boiled down to six simple words: "Don't Buy Stuff You Cannot Afford." The actors in the sketch could not grasp this simple concept, and it was both funny and sad to see them not understand the way to get out of debt, and the way to stay out of debt was to not spend money they didn't have.

Unfortunately, this is still true for many people, including those in the church.

In my counseling and research, I've seen where people don't have a clue about living on a plan for spending and managing their money. It's called a BUDGET.

Budgeting can seem mundane and boring—and frustrating and very restrictive. I really don't like the term "Budget." It makes me think of a diet or some form of medieval torture to pay for past sins. But when we begin to see what the spending plan is for, and how it is the major tool for achieving our financial goals, it can be exciting and life-giving.

Did Jesus have a spending plan? The Bible isn't clear, but I think so. There's nothing conclusive, but we could say He held money management and the idea of planned spending in high regard. He had a treasurer, of a sort—although it didn't work out too well, but He did assign the role.

In Luke 14, Jesus teaches the concept of planned spending in the context of intentional discipleship planning.

Luke 14:28–30 (NKJV)

"For which of you, intending to build a tower, does not sit down first and count the cost, whether he has enough to finish it—lest, after he has laid the foundation, and is not able to finish, all who see it begin to mock him, saying, 'This man began to build and was not able to finish?'"

God has said a lot in Scripture about planned spending and life planning in general.

Budgeting is nothing more than planning to spend money in an intentional way. Intentional means with purpose and according to a plan.

Even if you've never planned your finances before, chances are you have done planning in some fashion in your life. We spend our day with a plan and may not even realize it. We take our twenty-four hours and allocate it to things like sleep, work, chores around the house or activities with the kids. We plan our vacations and how we're going to spend the holidays. We plan how we're going to do our grocery run to do it most efficiently and not waste time. I never go to the grocery

> Budgeting is nothing more than planning to spend money in an intentional way.

store without some simple planning list—simply so I do not forget something. Ever forget to pay a bill due to not having it on the list?

The calendar is where we show this day planning (or on our Android, iPhone or in Outlook). Do you make shopping lists and to-do lists like I do? Do you write notes to remind yourself of appointments? Then you're planning your time like a spending plan.

If we do this with our time, why should we not plan how we're going to use our income?

The Bible has a lot to say about planning. God's heart is to plan. Didn't He create the universe in an orderly fashion?

> **Proverbs 16:1–3** (ESV)
> *The plans of the heart belong to man but the answer of the tongue is from the Lord. All the ways of man are pure in his own eyes, but the Lord weighs the spirit. Commit your work to the Lord, and your plans will be established.*

> **Proverbs 16:9** (ESV)
> *The heart of man plans his way, but the Lord establishes his steps.*

> **Proverbs 21:5** (ESV)
> *The plans of the diligent lead surely to abundance, but everyone who is hasty comes only to poverty.*

We really need to slow life down and plan. Recently, on a Saturday, I visited a car dealership, and before we even talked business, they wanted me to sign the paper that said I would buy the car that day if we came to terms. I would not sign it. It was all I could do to not be rude and walk out!

Another time, we were checking out a gym membership. The

salesman put us in a room and said the manager would be in to talk to us about special deals the facility was offering. The room was freezing cold. After what felt like an hour, the manager finally came in, he rattled off a series of deals, but his attitude informed us we had to decide that day or they would be off the table forever. I thought, *"Dude, my wife is about to take you out."*

High pressure tactics like these try to get us to buy now. And, too often, this kind of pressure leads to bad decisions. Take the time to pray and seek His guidance. And be ready to walk away from the deal.

Here is another planning scripture:

> **2 Chronicles 16:9** (NKJV)
> *For the eyes of the Lord run to and fro throughout the whole earth, to show Himself strong on behalf of those whose heart is loyal to Him.*

God is waiting for us to pause—to take a break—so He can get into our circumstances and do something on our behalf. If we are diligent in planning and slow in decision making, we create space for Him to have the opportunity to work.

Another good scripture on planning is Luke 16:10–11.

> *"Whoever can be trusted with very little can also be trusted with much, and whoever is dishonest with very little will also be dishonest with much. So if you have not been trustworthy in handling worldly wealth, who will trust you with true riches?"*

This works both for ministry and money. If you're faithful with little, you'll be faithful with much. And God will reward you.

IDEAL VERSUS REAL

We live in constant tension between the *ideal* and the *real*. We have our plan and where we want to go. That's the *ideal*. That tension between where we are and where we want to be can become so great we give up. We say, "I'm never gonna be where I want financially. So, why bother, it's hopeless." Or we look at the *real* in our lives right now and say, "I'm never gonna look how I wanna look, so pass me the bag of Oreos." I live in this world too.

My *ideal* includes items like:

> I want my home paid off.
> I want to have the entire Bible memorized.
> I want a perfect body.
> I want to be super-fast on my bicycle.
> I want to preach like Gateway Church's Senior Pastor, Robert Morris, and manage like our Senior Executive Pastor, Tom Lane! My financial ideal is to live on 1/3 of our income, save 1/3 and give 1/3.
> I want to be on Step 7 of the Route 7 Road Map.

My reality is that I do have a mortgage. My wife says I have an almost perfect body. We are working to get into our ideal financial plan.

I'm not where I want to be, but, praise God, I'm not where I once was. God isn't finished with me yet. And He's not finished with you either.

To get from where we are today (THE REAL) to where we want to be (THE IDEAL) takes a plan. It's not going to happen simply by wishing. It takes figuring out what we need to do to get where we want to be.

In Chapter 8, we'll discuss Life Stewardship and take on life planning. In this chapter, I want to focus on the basics of financial planning.

THE BASICS OF FINANCIAL PLANNING

When it comes to financial planning, people often get frustrated when their income doesn't match their outgo. They may give up and hope just to make it to the weekend or their next paycheck. Long-term planning goes out the window.

Let me encourage you. You *are* going to make it. It's all about taking baby steps and the incremental things we need to do to create a budget—a spending plan—we can actually live on. The decisions we make today will dictate where we end up tomorrow. This section on budgeting will help us make the wisest decisions to meet our goals.

While I was working in construction, I started a process of learning scriptures. I wanted to know where all the verses about money were located, and I wanted to memorize them. Years later, I connected this plan to my calling to be a pastor, to teach and counsel people from these exact scriptures. Through one thing after another, God showed me where I'm supposed to be. My willingness to make plans like this allowed Him the opportunity to work.

Whether you make $10,000 a year or over a million, it's all the same—you have to plan how you will spend your money.

There are some definite pros to a spending plan.

For one thing, you'll give yourself about a 20% pay raise when you carefully watch and manage your money. One man at my church told me he figured he would save over $300 a month if he brought his lunch from home instead of eating out with colleagues. As you pay attention, you'll find other little things that could add up to substantial savings. Make your coffee at home, and save all that money spent at "Bigbucks" coffee.

Living on a spending plan, you'll have better communication with your spouse. When you're planning the household spending, you have to communicate. When this happens, you end up on the same page and your household runs smoother. For my wife and I, money was our worst area of communication. We fought like cats and dogs over our finances. Today, it's our best area. We do not mind sitting down, going over our finances and planning what we need to do, what little tweaks we need to make to achieve our goals. Usually we get to buy items we have wanted personally because, working together, we see the money is there.

There is much less stress when you plan spending. When you plan and allocate your money, you're not worrying about using grocery money to pay your electric bill.

Spending plans will get you out of debt. As you put your plan together, and follow it, your debt will start to shrink. Make no mistake, it will be a process that takes time, but believe me, you will get there.

When you plan spending, you will see where you have room to increase your giving because you have a firmer handle on your finances.

With a spending plan, you will create more margin in your life. You'll gradually build a surplus and reach the point where you won't live paycheck-to-paycheck.

> There is much less stress when you plan spending.

You will eventually reach your financial goals.

You will slow down your spending decisions. A spending plan squashes impulse buying because you've got to look at the numbers. For example, my wife and I spent three months shopping for her car after deciding on the year, make and model before we found the one that fit our spending plan. Being patient saved us over $5000 dollars. In my household, that is worth the wait!

Managing your finances will highlight communication breakdowns. I see this happening among the departments at my church as budget discussions take place every budget season. Just like in a marriage, we see where people have been acting on assumptions because there hadn't been clear communication. A budget is a litmus test for how well you communicate.

Effective budgeting will require discipline in your life.

Finally, your lifestyle will change as you live by a budget. For example, when we committed to budgeting, I dropped the stop I would make at Dunkin' Donuts every morning. I switched to making coffee at home. And I hate making coffee—especially cleaning out the used grounds. But I made the change because I could see the value for our finances and our family.

What determines your intensity in the budgeting process? ***Don't miss this.*** The answer is determined by where you are in your calling. Your lifestyle decisions determine not only the direction you'll go, but also how intensely you'll pursue them.

When I was in construction, I was in good shape financially, but I was not on my calling. I needed to be intensely gung-ho on my financial plan at that time. If I hadn't been, if I hadn't purposely and enthusiastically adjusted my lifestyle down to a minimal level, despite having a strong income, I would not have been able to take the opportunity when God called me into full-time ministry.

In Chapter 4, we talked about the four stages of where you are in terms of your finances and your calling.

> Your lifestyle decisions determine not only the direction you'll go, but also how intensely you'll pursue them.

If you're on your calling and in good shape financially, that's great. Steady as you go.

If you're on your calling but *not* in good shape financially, that's okay. This book can help fix that.

If you're off your calling but in good shape financially, we can help with that as well. Not too long ago, I began counseling with a recently-retired businessman. He's in great shape financially but doesn't know how he should serve God during this season in his life. He and I are working together to find where God wants him to be, and it has given him more inspiration than any hobby he enjoyed.

If you're off your calling and in bad shape financially, you're in a tough season.

Here are three possible explanations for being off your calling and in bad financial shape. This could be a full teaching in itself, so I will only touch the highlights.

1. Wrong Attitudes

These are like having the incorrect address in our GPS system. No matter how hard we try to do the right things in our relationship with money, if we have greed, covetousness, deception, dishonesty, arrogance, pride, envy, fear, indulgence and pride giving us directions, we will only end up in pain or trouble.

> **Proverbs 28:25** *(emphasis added)*
> *The **greedy** stir up conflict, but those who trust in the Lord will prosper.*

> **1 Timothy 6:10**
> *For the love of money is a root of all kinds of evil. Some people, eager for money, have wandered from the faith and pierced themselves with many griefs.*

2. Bad Management

When our life calling and our finances are not managed, this is a partnership for complete frustration. To break this cycle, I recommend concentrating on two areas. First, is to get time with the Lord and ask Him about your calling, write down the impressions that come to your heart, and see if you can find a Scriptural reference for those impressions. After time with the Lord, seek counsel from trusted friends. Apply the lesson in Chapter 8 on Life Stewardship.

The second area is to really live on a spending plan. Get a financial coach who will hold you accountable. If your finances are a mess, know exactly why. No guessing anymore. When you can pinpoint the problem areas, you can then make wise decisions based on facts, not guesswork.

> **Proverbs 19:15** (NKJV)
> *Laziness casts one into a deep sleep, and an idle person will suffer hunger.*

> **Proverbs 20:13**
> *Do not love sleep or you will grow poor; stay awake and you will have food to spare.*

3. Course Adjustment

Sometimes, we go through rough times at no fault of our own and by no means do I desire to be one of Job's bad friends casting blame. In these dark days, there are always things God is showing us and maybe even new ministry efforts He is training us to lead. I understood more fully when I surrendered to my calling in the middle of major financial pain. Keep your ears open, your head on straight and press into a good church. You will make it.

The important thing is to keep all of this in perspective. Keep the big picture—your *ideal*—in front of you.

I see people so set on their goals, only to neglect other things in their lives, and they suffer all kinds of negative ramifications. I've counseled families who went crazy intense on their financial plan only to have major marital problems as a result of their over-the-top approach. A divorce destroys more than the financial plan.

I've seen couples stop having date nights. They worked so many hours, they didn't even see each other; they didn't have time. If you're working two or three jobs, you're losing time with your spouse and your kids. And you're headed towards serious health risks.

Are divorce or death really worth it? Bring some balance to your plan. A short season of ultra-intensity is good for you, but don't live there long-term.

Be really careful about putting your family in an unsafe $500 beater car just to get out of debt. Their safety is worth so much more than debt freedom. As a man who is good with wrenches, I have done the beater car for myself, but I would never do that to my wife and babies in the Dallas/Ft. Worth area. Intensity is good, but keep it all in perspective.

Don't break the Sabbath rest principle even if you have a fantastic plan. This is a violation of the Ten Commandments. I don't care how good your plan looks, working 100 hours per week will cost you much more than you could ever gain. God designed us to have rest. He even modeled it at Creation.

The Lord had to deal with me in this area. I was a workaholic, working seven days a week and wondering why there weren't more days in the week. Under His urging, I cut back to six days, then five. Working only five days a week in construction was unheard of in South Florida. Then He told me to cut back to four days a week and give one day to the church, serving in any capacity they asked me to.

"Lord," I said. "That's crazy. I can't run a construction company four days a week. If I'm not there, there will be mayhem. I've got projects lined up. I can't do this."

"Do you trust Me?"

How do you say no to that? I met with my pastor. He asked that I spend Thursdays counseling and doing Crown Ministry business.

I explained my schedule to the contractors I worked for. Sunday was dedicated to church, Saturday to my family and Thursday serving the church. The contractors paid me more to keep their projects a priority and to drop other builders. Looking back, I made more money being obedient to God and working four days a week than I ever did working seven.

I could feel God nudging me with His elbow. "Didn't I tell you? My ways are better than your ways."

> **Proverbs 3:5–6** (NKJV)
> *Trust in the Lord with all your heart, and lean not on your own understanding; in all your ways acknowledge Him, and He shall direct your paths.*

JESUS' MODEL FOR PLANNING

At the end of the day, our financial plans aren't that big of a deal. Yes, it is wise to seek God's wisdom and to exercise foresight in the management of our money, to set goals and targets, and to aim for them.

The big deal is, did I do the will of my Father? Will I hear, "Well done, good and faithful servant?" At the end of the day, all our plans, whether financial or career or ministry, should yield to God's plan for us.

Jesus describes this for us in John 6:38 (NKJV):

> *"For I have come down from heaven, not to do My own will, but the will of Him who sent me."*

His instruction to us makes this clear.

Matthew 6:9–10 (NKJV) *(emphasis added)*

*"In this manner, therefore pray: Our Father in heaven, hallowed be Your name. Your kingdom come. **Your will be done** on earth, as it is in heaven."*

Jesus' model is to do the Father's will—not His own will. This needs to be us as well. His will—not ours. We need to make the time to get with God and seek His will and His plan for our lives. Ask Him, "God, what is Your will for my life? What am I supposed to do? Where am I supposed to go?"

Jesus shows us this in action in His own life.

Luke 22:41–42 (NKJV)

And He was withdrawn from them about a stone's throw, and He knelt down and prayed, saying, "Father, if it is Your will, take this cup away from Me; nevertheless not My will, but Yours, be done."

The trump card in all planning is:

"Lord, what do You want me to do?"

"Where do I live?"

"Do we buy this house?"

"Do I take this job?"

"Do we homeschool, do private school or public school?"

Wrestle with all these questions that affect our Christian walk before the Lord. Listen for His voice. Follow His leading.

PRACTICAL APPLICATIONS

Spending Plan 101

Let's look at where we are and what steps we need to take.

First, estimate your location on the Route 7 Road Map. I've

found that, at this point in the process, almost everyone has to go back and fill in gaps in their spending plans. Planning is a fluid process. We're constantly learning new things, and we're seeing the effect of changes we are making and adjusting for those. We review to make sure we haven't missed anything and that we're still on track.

Then, get together with your spouse and discuss and list your goals. Write them down. The first time Missy and I did this, it felt a little silly to be asking my wife what her financial goals and dreams were. It was that uncomfortable feeling you have when you're doing something for the first time. I'm glad we did. We hit pay dirt as we shared our dreams and desires. Communication opened up and this list helped guide our decision making as the year went along.

Not too long ago, I was discussing this with a friend, helping him process the concepts I've been sharing. I asked him, "What is God doing in your life? How much is enough? Where are you going in your walk with the Lord?"

He answered, "I can't grow my business any larger and still do what God's called me to do. If I expand, I may make a little more money, but I'll lose the time I have to work for Him. It isn't worth it."

Nine months later, he called me. "I have this phenomenal opportunity to expand my business."

"Let me ask a question," I said. "What's changed in your goals; in the plans we discussed a few months ago?"

He hesitated. "That's a good question. You know, my wife and I have both had nagging feelings about this move. Her more than me, but you've confirmed what's been stirring in us. We're not going to go down that path. I'm not going to expand my business."

Setting goals and writing them down is so helpful in keeping us focused. To paraphrase Habakkuk 2:2, *"Write the vision."* If you haven't got it written down, how will you know what to aim for or when you've achieved it?

Next, determine your income. Figure out exactly how much you're bringing in.

Fourth, plan your spending for the month, but allocate by pay period using whatever tools work best for you. It could be the envelope method, YNAB (*youneedabudget.com*), MINT (*mint.com*), Quicken, spreadsheets or a combination of several—whatever gives you the best overview of both your income and your obligations. Then budget according to your pay period.

If you get paid every two weeks rather than twice a month, base your budget on two paychecks. Look at the math. If you get paid twice a month, you collect twenty-four checks in a year. If you get paid every two weeks, you get twenty-six checks. This is like an extra month's pay. It's a bonus. Don't spend it on everyday stuff. Earmark these extra checks for savings, your emergency fund or for getting out of debt.

If you're self-employed, you have to pay attention to the expense side of your budget so you'll know how much income you need to bring in.

Finally, at the end of the month, go back and balance your budget. See what happened to your money and make adjustments. Tools like YNAB and MINT, and even online banking, all have tools to help do this.

Spending Plan 201

This part of Route 7 is all about adjusting. Generally, about two or three months into the program, the plans don't look like we expected. This is not when we throw the plan away as a failure. This is when we go back and make adjustments, applying what we've learned about our finances, our lifestyles and about ourselves.

Dave Ramsey (*daveramsey.com*), Crown Ministries (*crown.org*) and Compass Ministry (*compass1.org*) all have excellent guidelines and charts to show how to allocate our income by percentage (so much for housing, clothing, food, etc.).

Remember, these are recommendations. Your percentages don't have to match what they suggest. But it is very helpful to allocate your income by percentage. It helps to quickly show if some area is out of whack.

Monthly Spending Plan

Categories	Actual From Register	% of Gross Income	Guideline %	Guideline Amount	Budget Amount
Net Income					
Giving (Tithe, Offerings)					
Food	0.00				0.00
Groceries					
Restaurants					
Housing	0.00				0.00
Mortgage/Rent					
Electricity/Gas					
Water					
Telephone/Cell Phone					
Internet/TV Service					
Maintenance & Repairs					
House/Rental Insurance					
Taxes					
Other					
Miscellaneous	0.00				0.00
Gifts					
Other					
Personal	0.00				0.00
Health/Life/Disability Premiums					
Health Out-of-Pocket Expenses					
Flexible Spending Account					
Hair Care					
Clothing					
Recreation	0.00				0.00
His	0.00				
Hers					
Entertainment					
Vacation					
Transportation	0.00				0.00
Car Payment					
Gas					
Car Insurance					
License/Registration					
Maintenance & Repairs					
Savings					
Child Exp (Tuition, Lessons, Day Care)					
Debt (Credit Card, Student Loans, etc.)					
Net Income - Expenses	0.00	#DIV/0!	0%	$0.00	0.00

A couple came in to see me for counseling, and one of the first things they said was, "We love our house." The problem was since they'd bought it three years earlier, they had run up $36,000 in credit card debt. The first thing I looked at was the house. In 2007, they had taken out a $550,000 variable rate, interest only mortgage without escrowing property taxes or insurance. They earned $60,000 per year. They got into the house by taking a non-qualifying loan and using an inheritance check as a down payment. The mortgage lender did not verify their income.

Every month, they were short at least $2,500 dollars.

I took out one of the percentage charts and showed them where 74% of their spendable income was being spent on their house. They had a house they couldn't afford.

I was prepared to play the bad guy (the meanie), but as we went over the numbers and the percentages, they came to the realization on their own. They were in way over their heads with too much house for their income. All on their own, they decided to sell.

When looking at these percentage guidelines, don't see them as rigid, never-to-be-violated rules. You can be over in some areas and under in others to balance it out. For example, some people have a lifestyle where they eat out a lot, way over the recommended percentages. But their house is paid off, so the percentage of their income that goes for housing is much less than the guideline suggests.

After you've figured out how to use the percentages to their best advantage, align your goals with Route 7 and with your calling. If you're not in that sweet spot in your calling yet, look at your numbers and figure out how to increase your margin. Then, when the opportunity arises, you'll be in the position to move into that new area God has planned for you.

If your income is less than your budget, you need to get creative in your planning. Remember the three options we outlined earlier: Make More Money, Spend Less Money or Sell Stuff. As we noted, spending less is the most effective option for getting into balance. *Remember: "Don't Buy Stuff You Cannot Afford."*

What if you're in a financial crisis? For several years, I handled benevolence at our church and daily dealt with people in crisis.

The first thing to do is stop and pray.

One day, this single mother came to see me. Her husband had taken a job as a streetside pharmaceutical supplier—he was dealing drugs. He was arrested and, in Florida, you lose your car immediately. They were a one-car family. He was a multiple offender. This was his third strike, and he was facing a mandatory ten-year sentence.

I told her we had to pray. She looked at me like I was crazy. I told her we needed to get God in the situation to help bail her out. So we prayed for a car for her, and I could tell she didn't really believe me, but I used my faith to stand in the gap for her.

Almost immediately, she received a phone call from her mother who had used her income tax refund to buy her daughter a car and was driving it down from Michigan.

The next thing to do after you pray is get counsel. When we're in a crisis, we tend to get tunnel vision. We don't see the whole picture, and our focus may not be where it should be. Counseling will help you see different viewpoints and give you ideas you didn't see before. Plus, counseling helps you connect with a bigger group of people and more options will open up.

I've seen crises resolved in Life Groups because of the connections that are made in those small, caring gatherings.

> When we're in a crisis, we tend to get tunnel vision.

Third, plan your financial moves very, very carefully. Meet your basic needs of food, transportation and housing first. Then live on a shoestring budget with the rest of the money, stretching it as far as it will go. Be creative and be ready to make hard decisions.

Notice, I didn't include debt in the above paragraph. If you're in crisis, I don't want you paying a Master Card bill if you don't have enough food for your family.

1 Timothy 5:8 tells us that those who don't take care of their family are worse than unbelievers.

Finally, over-communicate with your creditors. Keep in touch with them regularly. When you initiate contact and explain your difficulties, they frequently don't know what to do with you. They're used to people running away from them. You're coming to them. They're more likely to be cooperative when this happens.

Use Dave Ramsey's Pro Rata Plan. Pro Rata means "Fair Share" plan. On your shoestring budget, take what you have left over that you could send to a creditor. Divide it up based on the percentage you owe each creditor and send it out. It won't be a full payment, but it will be something. This method recognizes you know you need to pay off your debts. But when you're in a crisis, these small payments will buy you some time until you're on your feet again and can fully meet your obligations.

Pay your secured debts first. Then pay your unsecured debt like your credit cards. These unsecured debt holders will call you quickly and can be nasty and ugly. This is one of the areas where it works best to contact them first and stay in communication with them to let them know you're not ignoring your debt.

There's a book called *Money Troubles* put out by an organization called NOLO which means "Law for All." It has some suggested form letters to use when communicating with creditors. Dave Ramsey also has similar letters on his website.

CARS

One of the keys to being successful in Route 7 is to get out of automobile debt and stay out. It's a process that will take time, but it is so worth it. Here are five steps to conquer the car monster.

Step One
Keep your car for three years after the loan is paid off. If you have a four-year note on your car, plan on keeping it seven years—at least.

Step Two
Include the car payment in your debt snowball, and knock it out as quickly as you can.

Step Three
After the car is paid off, continue to make the car payments. Only pay them to yourself, not the creditor. Set them aside in a separate account as the New Car account so you won't be tempted to spend them on the big screen TV.

Step Four
Use this saved cash plus your car to purchase a newer used car.

Step Five
Repeat the process of saving and upgrading. Keep making the car payment to yourself and saving it, and soon you'll be paying cash for an excellent used car.

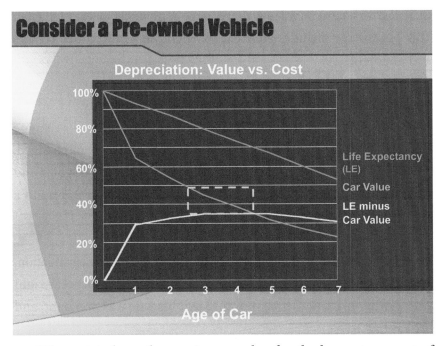

We want to have the maximum value for the longest amount of time. This plan will get us there and keep us there.

It's not always wrong to buy a brand new car, but because of rapid depreciation, it's seldom wise. I advise you that if you want to buy a brand new car, plan on driving it at least ten years so you can recoup your cost.

Today's cars will last fifteen to twenty years. But we pay for them at the beginning, and then all the depreciation happens. If we drive it for only five years or less, we've lost a lot of the value of that car. On average, a person drives a new car for around four years.

In my counseling experiences, I've discovered a lot of mistakes people make with their cars.

TOP 10 CAR MISTAKES

Mistake One – People don't plan or budget for their car.

The automobile category of your financial plan should be no more than 15–18%, depending on where you live and how much you drive.

In Texas, for example, we may drive more and our cars wear out faster. This percentage includes your car payment, insurance, fuel, repairs and maintenance.

Mistake Two – People don't maintain their cars properly.
A lady complained to me once about her Honda Accord whose engine blew up at 50,000 miles. It turned out she had never had the oil changed. She misunderstood what the dealer told her when she bought it and never read the Owner's Manual. Find a good mechanic and build a relationship with him (or her).

Mistake Three – Sometimes people buy the wrong car for their situation. I had a friend who bought an expensive two-seater sports car right after getting married. Three months later, his wife was pregnant, and the car had to go.

Another friend bought a Dodge Hemi truck, and he loved that truck. He lived in Fort Worth and worked in North Dallas. His commute was around one hundred miles per day. The truck got 10 MPG. The cost of gas alone was eating up his income. He'd have been better off to have bought a Corolla and slap a Hemi decal on the side of it.

Mistake Four – Not getting a pre-purchase inspection by *your* mechanic *(see Mistake Two)*.
One time, Missy and I found a Suburban we were looking for. It met our expectations to the letter. Before we signed for it, I brought it to my mechanic for an inspection. He told us not to buy the vehicle. The frame was rusted out and had been sandblasted and repainted to disguise the damage. His concern was the car would fold up like a cardboard box in a wreck.

Mistake Five – Letting the car dealer bully you.

I'm sure you've experienced being with a salesman who puts you in a little room while he goes to talk with the sales manager about the deal because "he's got the numbers." Follow him into the manager's office. Tell the manager, "Here's what I want to pay. Call me when you're ready to talk numbers."

Mistake Six – Bad financing.

Avoid getting financing through the dealer. The objective is to get the car paid off without paying a ton of interest. You want to get the lowest interest rate you can for the shortest term you can afford in your budget and pay it off early. Put your financing together on your own through a local credit union.

Several years ago, I went to a dealer to buy a *new* used car. I found the right car, and the finance office wanted to charge me 20% interest because of my credit score (which was high 700s by the way)! I went to another dealer and bought the same exact car at 4% interest.

Mistake Seven – Co-signing.

Never, never, never, ever co-sign a loan for anyone, especially family. Co-signing is backing someone else's credit. If they had any credit, they wouldn't need a co-signer. Don't co-sign for your children. Let them drive something a little older. Let them put some skin in this game and really work at this thing.

Scripture backs this up.

> **Proverbs 17:18** (ESV)
> *One who lacks sense gives a pledge and puts up security in the presence of his neighbor.*

Proverbs 22:26–27 (ESV)
Be not one of those who give pledges, who put up security for debts. If you have nothing with which to pay, why should your bed be taken from under you?

Proverbs 11:15 (ESV)
Whoever puts up security for a stranger will surely suffer harm, but he who hates striking hands in pledge is secure.

But, Pastor Gunnar, what if I've already co-signed a loan?
Get out of it!
Look at Proverbs 6:1–5 (ESV)
My son, if you have put up security for your neighbor, have given your pledge for a stranger, if you are snared in the words of your mouth, caught in the words of your mouth, then do this, my son, and save yourself, for you have come into the hand of your neighbor: go, hasten, and plead urgently with your neighbor. Give your eyes no sleep and your eyelids no slumber; save yourself like a gazelle from the hand of the hunter, like a bird from the hand of the fowler.

Pastor Gunnar's paraphrase: *Go nuts until you can get out of that co-signing deal.*
I would rather give them the car. If you can't do that, don't co-sign.

Mistake Eight – Selling too soon or too late.
My goal is to drive a car as economically as possible, between five cents and twenty-five cents per mile. I have a simplified formula for looking at the car.

Take the purchase price of the car PLUS the maintenance and repair expenses (not gas or insurance), MINUS what I sell the car for, DIVIDED by the miles I drove it. This gives me the cost per mile.

Purchase Price	$10,700
Repairs and Maintenance	$1,400
Total	$12,100
Estimated Sales Price	$9,500
My Cost	$2,600
Divided by Miles Driven	25,000
Equals Cost per Mile	.104 per mile

Mistake Nine – The leasing trap.

Most of the time leasing is a very expensive way, if not *the* most expensive way, to drive a car. When you lease, you pay for the depreciation over and over again. Dealers like it because not only do they profit from your lease payments, when the lease is over, they have a very nice, well-maintained car for their used-car market. One they can sell for a higher price than a non-leased car.

Mistake Ten – Buying the car when there's been no prayer about it, there is no peace, and if you're married, there is no unity with your **spouse.**

Another simple formula for you:

No prayer PLUS no peace PLUS no unity EQUALS no purchase.

No matter how good the deal looks, walk away.

CHAPTER SIX

THE SAVING PLAN

Let me share with you an example from Chuck Missler of how, sometimes, significant things can be hidden in Scripture. No, this isn't going to be a message on deciphering secret number codes or strange doctrines. I want to show you how God can string things together to teach us profound truths.

Look at Genesis, Chapter 5. This is a genealogy, and I want to look at the names because each name has a meaning in Hebrew. And the meanings have a message for us.

Adam means "man."

Seth, his son, means "appointed."

Enosh, Seth's son, means "mortal" or "frail." Enosh's generation is the first time in history when people began to rebel against the Lord.

Kenan, Enosh's son, means "sorrow" or "dirge."

Mahalalel, Kenan's son, means "blessed" or "praise." Any time you see "el" in a name, it means the name of God is buried in that name. For example, Dani**el** means God is my judge. Nathani**el** means "gift of God."

Jared, Mahalalel's son, means "shall come down."

Enoch, Jared's son, means "teaching" or "commencement." He was the first of four generations of teachers.

Methuselah, Enoch's son, means "his death shall bring forth." Methuselah was the oldest man ever. He is a representation of the extensiveness of God's mercy and the slowness of His wrath. God promised He would not flood the earth until Methuselah was gone.

Lamech, Methuselah's son, means "lament" or "lamentation."

Noah, Lamech's son, means "to bring relief" or "comfort."

All this is, I'm sure, edifying on some level, but let's see what it looks like when we bring them all together.

Hebrew	English
Adam	Man
Seth	Appointed
Enosh	Mortal
Kenan	Sorrow
Mahalalel	The Blessed God
Jared	Shall come down
Enoch	Teaching
Methuselah	His death shall bring
Lamech	he despairing
Noah	Rest or comfort

In English, it reads "Man appointed mortal sorrow. The Blessed God shall come down teaching that His death shall bring the despairing rest or comfort."

Even in genealogies, God speaks to us with His message of love and comfort.

THE SAVING PLAN

This chapter was a challenge to prepare. As I thought about it and pulled the various parts together, it created questions that I wrestled with. Some of the questions were:

Does saving show a lack of faith?

Am I a fool for not saving?

How much should I save?

How do I guard against hoarding and greed?

With so many starving in the world, as a Christian, what's my balance between giving and saving and all these other options I have with living on the money God's given me?

As we explore this whole idea of saving as a Christian, I think you'll discover the right balance.

Pastor Bob Coy of Calvary Chapel in Fort Lauderdale gave this example of putting the people of the world into perspective.

Let's look at the world as made up of 100 people.

- *70 of them don't know Jesus. 30 do.*
- *30 are white (or vanilla). 70 are some other flavor.*
- *51 are women, 49 are men.*
- *80 live in substandard housing, meaning they have no electricity, running water, inside plumbing or a roof over their head.*
- *50 are malnourished. Their food is not satisfying, not enough and doesn't provide proper nutrition.*
- *70 can't read.*
- *1 is dying as you read this—a little kid under the age of 10. He's dying because he can't get enough to eat.*
- *6 have a significant portion of the world's wealth.*
- *6 live in the United States.*
- *What if you're the dad of the kid who's dying of malnourishment? Wouldn't you be asking one of the 6 wealthy to share a little for*

your child? Unfortunately, the answer all too often is: there's other things to do with our money, new things to buy.

It can seem even worse when we look at how Americans use money.

- *24% goes for housing.*
- *19% goes for health care (insurance, prescriptions, cold medicines, health club memberships).*
- *22% goes for recreation and personal needs—what we do for fun.*
- *15% goes for food.*
- *17% goes for transportation.*

Does that leave anything for the kid on the other side of the world who's dying? Non-Christians around the world give around 2% to organizations that may make a difference in that kid's life. If you're a Christian, that number skyrockets all the way to 3%.

If you look at Americans from the outside, you'll see we don't live on a balanced budget. This isn't just the government. It's the people as well. We spend a heck of a lot more than we bring in. Individuals and families are rapidly increasing their debt load because of the belief we don't have enough stuff. And we are a large part of the 1/6 of people in the world who have all the resources.

When I look at the statistics, I can't help but think of the opportunity we, as the Church, have for massive influence. But where do we begin? We begin by going to God and asking Him to help us to find balance. Ask for His perspective on saving, giving and how we balance all this out. How do we help bring rest and comfort to those who are despairing?

This weighs heavy on me at times, but I'm comforted knowing God is not caught off guard. We didn't catch Him by surprise. He has put everything we need in Scripture.

The answer isn't forced socialism or forced giving. The answer lies in people who are open to the things of God and who choose to live generous lives in Christ.

Philippians 4:11–14 says:

For I have learned to be content whatever the circumstances. I know what it is to be in need, and I know what it is to have plenty. I have learned the secret of being content in any and every situation, whether well fed or hungry, whether living in plenty or in want. I can do all things through Christ who gives me strength.

Join me in this prayer before we continue.

Father, how do we balance saving, living and giving? What does Your Scripture say to us as wealthy Christians in a blessed country living in a hurting and dying world? How do we make an impact?

Lord, I'm begging—show us how to do this. Bless us as we search out Your Word and find sense in Your teaching.

Holy Spirit, we invite You to be our Teacher. In Christ's name. Amen.

ASCETICISM AND MATERIALISM

There are two sides to this coin we've been discussing.

Asceticism is the side most of our forerunners in faith have leaned toward. This philosophy continues in some circles even today. Curiously, it may not have a solid Biblical basis or foundation.

Asceticism describes a lifestyle characterized by abstinence from various worldly pleasures, often with the aim of pursuing religious and spiritual goals. Christian authors such as Origen, Jerome and Augustine interpreted Biblical texts within a highly asceticized religious environment.

My overly simplistic interpretation of some of what they taught is: "I'm going to deny myself." To be holy was to be absolutely poor, to shun material goods.

There are some well-meaning teachers today who teach asceticism, to get rid of all material possessions in our Christian life.

In studying this, I read a story about Mother Teresa. She and her group received a gift that included a home to help people. The home had carpet, hot water and other amenities. And Mother Teresa and her people pulled them all out. They turned off the hot water and removed the carpet because they didn't want to have anything that was comfortable. They felt it was presuming too much on God. That was the way they did their ministry.

When I studied the ascetics, my first thought was, "Lord, I'm just going to give it all away."

I was comforted when He said to me, "Maybe that's not what I'm asking you to do. Maybe that's not what I'm asking you to teach."

Sometimes, a person receives a revelation from the Lord for their own, personal lifestyle, and they think they need to apply it across the board to EVERYONE else. It probably wasn't meant for everyone else, just adjustments God wanted them to make in their own life.

The Bible provides guiding principles for how to live, but God never comes out and says, "This way is exactly how to live." I think He leaves it that way for us to wrestle in our hearts: *Lord, what are You asking me to do? What's my role in all this?*

Asceticism is wrong in several areas. Scripture does not teach that poverty is godliness. Both the poor and the wealthy need a Savior. In my experience running benevolence, I've run into greedy, selfish and sinful poor people. That may be politically incorrect, but they do exist. It's a condition of the heart. It's an issue we all deal with regardless of our income level.

Asceticism doesn't create godliness within somebody. We all have a need for Jesus no matter what our income level is.

Asceticism can also be a form of pride. If you are "showing off" your lack of material possessions to be praised by men, this is self-righteous pride.

> We all have a need for Jesus no matter what our income level is.

A group of Buddhists live near us at a temple set back off the main road. I've seen them walking barefoot in the cold. But I have also seen them waiting at the bus stop on their cell phones, and I ran across them in the Apple Store with their iPads and iPhones. I'm not judging them in any way. I just thought it was funny to see the contrast.

Matthew 6:1–2 (NKJV)
"Take heed that you do not do your charitable deeds before men, to be seen by them. Otherwise, you have no reward from your Father in heaven. Therefore, when you do a charitable deed, do not sound a trumpet before you as the hypocrites do in the synagogues and in the streets, that they may have glory from men. Assuredly, I say to you, they have their reward."

If you give something away, don't do it in a way that will draw attention or bring notice to you.

When I was young in ministry, I thought it holy as a stewardship pastor to drive really cheap junk cars. If it started, I drove it. My goal was to drive stuff that didn't cost me more than $300. My wife hated it. I think I embarrassed her. They always leaked something on the driveway. They even occasionally caught on fire! Once, I had an Olds Cutlass whose vinyl roof was torn. Air would catch in it as I drove. Not only did it look ridiculous, it cut my gas mileage to single digits. I did this because I thought it made me look more spiritual or godly. It was just another form of pride.

I have since repented and bought a nicer car.

Jesus was not an ascetic, but I do believe He was very strategic. He experienced being poor and having poor friends. Yet, He was also criticized for his party friends—people who had money and who liked to celebrate.

Matthew 11:19 described Jesus in this way:

"The Son of Man came eating and drinking, and they say,

'Here is a glutton and a drunkard, a friend of tax collectors and sinners.' But wisdom is proved by her deeds."

Jesus had wealthy friends such as Joseph of Arimathea, Mary, Martha, Lazarus, Nicodemus and Zacchaeus. Luke was a physician, Matthew a tax collector and many of the disciples were successful businessmen owning boats and homes and having servants.

He was comfortable with the upper crust folks of His day. He never rebuked people for having stuff. He only rebuked them for not being generous *with* their stuff.

Materialism is just as dangerous as asceticism, only from the other extreme. The theory behind materialism is that the only thing that exists is matter or energy; all things are composed of material and material interactions. It's the thought that everything I can see and feel—that's the genuine reality.

Our culture is very materialistic, and this world view has snuck into the church and created issues and problems among believers. Actually, materialism runs rampant in the church, and I believe it's why the body of Christ is so ungenerous as a whole.

I think Christians only give 3% because we've slipped into these materialistic pitfalls.

Pastor Robert Morris made the observation that people are comfortable saying God owns everything, but when we mention tithing 10%, they get upset and angry. It touches a nerve when you go from concept to application. All of a sudden, God may not own everything. "You want some of it? No way; it's MINE!"

> Our culture is very materialistic, and this world view has snuck into the church.

Materialism is greed, and it's rooted in the spirit of mammon. This spirit can drive both materialism and asceticism because it also operates in the area of pride.

MAMMON

Mammon is an Aramaic word meaning riches. It comes from the Syrian god of riches. This god is rooted in Babylon which means "sown in confusion." And Babylon comes from the Tower of Babel. Mammon is a prideful, arrogant spirit that says, "We don't need God."

Mammon is the spirit that rests on money that is not submitted to God. All money has one of two spirits on it. Mammon is on money that is not submitted to God; people use money to replace God.

Money that has been submitted to God and does not try to replace Him, but serves Him, is blessed. That's why *this* money grows and multiplies and is not devoured by the devourer.

One of the ways mammon manifests itself is through greed.

Greed is the inordinate desire to possess wealth, goods or objects of abstract value with the intention of keeping it for oneself, far beyond the dictates of basic survival and comfort.

Greed is the unholy fruit of the spirit of mammon.

Jesus gives some perspective in a group of scriptures that we all know but maybe never put them together. In the passage, Jesus is talking about leveraging resources today for Kingdom opportunities after He has shared the story of the shrewd manager in Chapter 16 of Luke's Gospel. Let's pick it up in verses 9–15.

> **Luke 16:9–15**
> *"I tell you, use worldly wealth to gain friends for yourselves, so that when it is gone, you will be welcomed into eternal dwellings. Whoever can be trusted with very little can also be trusted with much, and whoever is dishonest with very little will also be dishonest with much. So if you have not been trustworthy in handling worldly wealth, who will trust you with true riches? And if you have not been trustworthy*

with someone else's property, who will give you property of your own? No one can serve two masters. Either you will hate the one and love the other, or you will be devoted to the one and despise the other. You cannot serve both God and money." The Pharisees, who loved money, heard all this and were sneering at Jesus. He said to them, "You are the ones who justify yourselves in the eyes of others, but God knows your hearts. What people value highly is detestable in God's sight."

Jesus is showing us that it's a heart test. How much we save, how much we keep is all a test of the heart. If we can't give it away, no matter what the value, we fail the test.

Here are some examples.

Mark 10:21–22

Jesus looked at him and loved him. "One thing you lack," he said. "Go, sell everything you have and give to the poor, and you will have treasure in heaven. Then come follow me." At this the man's face fell. He went away sad, because he had great wealth.

At this point, the rich young ruler has failed the heart test. He may have passed it later, but it wasn't recorded.

Genesis 22:2–3

Then God said, "Take your son, your only son, whom you love—Isaac—and go to the region of Moriah. Sacrifice him there as a burnt offering on a mountain I will show you."

And what did Abraham do? Early the next morning, Abraham

got up and loaded his donkey.

This is interesting because there's no record of Abraham pushing back. Remember the story of Sodom and Gomorrah? Abraham pushed back five times as he bargained with God over how many righteous men it would take to save the cities.

Over the years, his heart had softened, and his faith grew stronger. He had experienced so much of God's blessing, he may have thought, *"Okay. It sounds like a crazy idea, but I'll do it."* He was ready to do whatever God told him to do. Abraham heard God and was obedient.

I wonder how many people hearing Abraham's story may have attempted the same, *NOT* hearing from God with tragic results.

Luke 12:16–21 has one more example.

> *And he told them this parable: "The ground of a certain rich man yielded an abundant harvest. He thought to himself, 'What shall I do? I have no place to store my crops.'*
> *Then he said, 'This is what I'll do. I will tear down my barns and build bigger ones, and there I will store my surplus grain. And I'll say to myself, "You have plenty of grain laid up for many years. Take life easy; eat, drink and be merry."'*
> *But God said to him, 'You fool! This very night your life will be demanded from you. Then who will get what you have prepared for yourself?' This is how it will be with whoever stores up things for themselves but is not rich toward God."*

The fool wasn't chastised for saving up. He was chastised for not being rich toward God.

I think these verses have been taught incorrectly in the past. God may have given him bigger barns as a strategic resource for something else God wanted him to do. Saving money and possessions is not a problem with God. The problem arises when we refuse to release what God has given us because our heart is too tangled up in it.

Here are some scriptures on saving as we prepare to move forward on Route 7.

1 Corinthians 16:2 (NASB)
On the first day of every week each one of you is to put aside and save, as he may prosper, so that no collections be made when I come.

Proverbs 6:6–8 (NKJV)
Go to the ant, you sluggard! Consider her ways and be wise, which, having no captain, overseer or ruler, provides her supplies in the summer, and gathers her food in the harvest.

Proverbs 21:20 (LB)
The wise man saves for the future but the foolish man spends whatever he gets.

Proverbs 27:12 (NASB)
A prudent man sees evil and hides himself, the naive proceed and pay the penalty.

Proverbs 30:24–25 (NASB)
Four things are small on the earth, but they are exceedingly wise: The ants are not a strong people, but they prepare their food in the summer.

Ecclesiastes 11:2 (NASB)
Divide your portion to seven, or even to eight, for you do not know what misfortune may occur on earth.

Several years ago, I had a neighbor who worked for Enron. I always like to ask people what they do for a living because I know they'll ask me the same question. That opens the door for me to talk about church and Biblical stewardship, which is something I know they always want to hear about.

This neighbor asked, kind of sarcastically, if the Bible said anything on investing. I quoted Ecclesiastes 11:2. He thought that was interesting and cool, but he had all his money in Enron stock because they gave a good match.

"You know that violates Biblical principles," I said.

"Yeah, but it's a big company with a good track record."

Well, a short time later, the whole company fell apart, and he lost the majority of his portfolio.

> **Proverbs 30:8–9**
>
> *Give me neither poverty nor riches, but give me only my daily bread, otherwise, I may have too much and disown you and say, "Who is the Lord?" Or I may become poor and steal, and so dishonor the name of my God.*

Here's a quick recap of what we've been discussing in this chapter:
Not saving violates God's Word.
*Poverty **does not** make us more godly.*
Materialism is a spiritual cancer and a mask for a greedy heart.

Follow God in whatever He asks you to do because we are HIS stewards. Sometime, He'll have you save aggressively to do something with it while at other times it may not be so aggressive. You need to work it out with Him through prayer and wise counsel.

PRACTICAL APPLICATIONS
Route 7 Review
Step One
Start tithing and giving firstfruits (Proverbs 3:9–10).

Create our monthly spending plan (Luke 14:28–30).

Adjust our lifestyle (Proverbs 23:4–5).

Save $1,000 for our emergency fund (Proverbs 21:20).

Step Two

Start giving offerings (Mark 14:3–7).

Pay off all credit cards and high interest loans (Proverbs 22:7).

Start storehouse savings (Proverbs 21:5). *(I'll get back to this.)*

Step Three

Increase giving percentage (2 Corinthians 9:6–14).

Pay off all loans (Psalm 37:21).

Increase storehouse savings to three months (Proverbs 30:24–25).

Step Four

Create strategic giving plan (1 Corinthians 16:2).

Create strategic storehouse savings plan (1 Timothy 6:6).

Short-term goal: car replacement, home upgrades, college (Proverbs 28:20).

Mid-term goal: one-year living expenses (Proverbs 6:6–8).

Long-term income replacement.

Step Five

Continue strategic giving plan (Proverbs 28:22).

Calling evaluation: back to college, start business, career change (1 Timothy 6:7–10).

Investment stage: Build assets that create cash flow (Ecclesiastes 11:2).

Pre-pay mortgage (Proverbs 28:19). *(Pre-pay your mortgage after you've established a firm financial foundation.)*

Step Six

Continue strategic giving plan (2 Corinthians 9:6–14).

Pay off mortgage (Romans 13:8).

Step Seven

Extravagant generosity (2 Corinthians 9:6–14).

100% strategic living (1 Timothy 6:17–19).

Storehouse Savings

Storehouse savings is a cool concept. Think of it as a barn with multiple sections for storing goods—or for our purposes, money.

Each section is designated for a specific purpose. One could be for college savings, another for the emergency fund, still another for the car payment we're making to ourselves. Missy and I are saving for specific items, so we set money aside in an account designated for those purposes. This way, we're not as likely to give into the temptation to use it for something else. And it also helps us track our savings and giving goals.

God is very strong on storehouses.

> **Genesis 41:56** *(emphasis added)*
> *When the famine had spread over the whole country, Joseph opened all the **storehouses** and sold grain to the Egyptians, for the famine was severe throughout Egypt.*

In the time of plenty, God told Joseph to build storehouses all over Egypt to store grain for the famine times, to build a place to draw from.

God has storehouses. Deuteronomy 28:12 tells us: "The Lord will open the heavens, the **storehouse** of his bounty, to send rain on your land in season and to bless all the work of your hands. You will lend to many nations but will borrow from none." *(emphasis added)*

Here's a scripture I claim for myself and I urge you to do so, too.

> **Deuteronomy 28:8** (NLT) *(emphasis added)*
> *"The Lord will guarantee a blessing on everything you do and will fill your **storehouses** (more than one) with grain. The Lord your God will bless you in the land he is giving you."*

Ten Tips for Saving

People have asked me how to create a margin for saving. Here are ten tips for saving.

Tip 1

Save second; pay God first. I've noticed in my own experience and in counseling, that when we pay God last, there's not much left for Him. So we pay Him first and pay ourselves second.

Tip 2

Use auto draft to direct deposit. We don't see the money so we're not tempted to touch it. It goes directly into whatever account we've designated for whatever purpose. And we need to make adjustments and tweak it, as our income increases and we achieve financial goals.

Tip 3

Be consistent. It's amazing how much we save when we are consistent about it.

Tip 4

Save for different purchases rather than one big pile. Divide up your savings accounts into different categories. Or set up separate accounts.

Tip 5

Set up different accounts and even in different banks. This really helps us leave the money alone. We make it a hassle to have to touch it. It gives us time to think over our options.

Tip 6

Move all our raises to savings and "flatline" our lifestyle. When we determine to live on a certain amount, any raises or extra income we get can go directly into savings. Missy and I are living on the income we had four years ago. All my raises go into savings.

Tip 7

Pray about savings. Seek His wisdom and guidance as to how much we should save.

Tip 8

Give from our savings, not our regular budget.

Tip 9

Add any decrease in our monthly expenses to our savings. For example, after shopping around, I was able to cut our car insurance premium in half. All that extra money went into savings.

Tip 10

Save as we pay off debt. As we pay off a debt, add that money to savings to avoid going back into debt when something breaks. This requires steady plodding, but it is so worth it. $1,000 isn't much of an emergency fund these days.

CHAPTER SEVEN

DEBT

Let me be up front with you: I hate debt! I see debt as a form of bondage that keeps us tied to the lender and interferes with accomplishing all God desires for us. The stress of debt leads to fear, poor communication, poor decision making and damaged relationships—sometimes beyond repair.

If you are struggling with debt, I have no desire to condemn you, but I want to help you get free. Walk with me as I unpack the Biblical view of debt and give some options for you to personalize a plan to get out.

WHAT IS DEBT?

As always in this book, let's establish our scriptural foundation. Here are some Merriam-Webster dictionary definitions of five different words associated with and around debt. The key is to study and see what the Bible actually says.

Debt is something owed. Anyone having borrowed money or goods from another owes a debt and is under obligation to return the goods or repay the money, usually with interest.

In Nehemiah's time (Nehemiah 5:1–5), things were a mess in Israel. He was trying to rebuild the walls and foreigners opposed him. On top of that, the people were crying out because of the debt they were forced to bear. *"We are mortgaging our fields, our vineyards and our houses that we might get grain because of the famine."* They were borrowing to keep from starving.

"We have borrowed money for the king's tax on our field and our vineyards." They borrowed money to pay their taxes.

They were forcing their sons and daughters into slavery to pay off debt. They felt helpless because their fields and vineyards belonged to others. Children were placed into slavery to pay off debt.

This in no way was or is God's intention.

Sounds like tough times, but that can't happen in our modern day, right? There are many modern parallels. In many parts of our world, children are sold into sex trafficking to pay off family debts. Then the economic crises of Cyprus, Greece, Spain and Portugal look strangely similar to the Israelites in Nehemiah's day. While those nations are not in the position of selling off family members to cover debts, they are in the process of making deep, painful cuts to survive the crushing debt.

What gives me great concern is the speed at which the United States is following in their footsteps with our out-of-control debt.

I digress back to scripture. In Matthew 18:26–33, Jesus tells us of the unmerciful servant. His master forgave him a huge debt, yet the servant turned around and demanded another servant pay him a niggling little debt or be thrown into prison. Debt can distort our values and our sense of justice and compassion.

God identifies the qualities of a righteous man as including restoring the debtor to his pledge and one who does not lend money on interest. Such a man is righteous and will surely live. (Ezekiel 18:7–9).

Borrowing is taking and using something that belongs to someone else with the intention of returning it. It also includes borrowing money with the intent of repaying the money plus interest.

The Lord doesn't mind borrowing—as long as we're not the ones on the borrowing side. He describes being a lender as a blessing.

Deuteronomy 15:6 (NASB)
"You will not borrow; and you will rule over many nations but they will not rule over you."

Deuteronomy 28:12 (NASB)
"You shall lend to many nations, but you shall not borrow."

Proverbs 22:7 (NASB)
The borrower becomes the lender's slave.

Surety is a word we don't hear too much anymore, but the concept is very alive in today's society. I'm in surety when I have become legally responsible for the debt, default or failure of another. We call it *co-signing*, usually for someone's car or personal note.

God is real clear about this.

Proverbs 22:26 (NASB)
Do not be among those who give pledges, among those who become guarantors for debts.

Earlier in Proverbs 6:1–4 (NLT), the Lord advises, *"If you've already co-signed, get out of it as quickly as possible. If you have been caught by the words of your mouth … deliver yourself. Since you have come into the hand of your neighbor, go, humble yourself, and importune your neighbor."*

When co-signing goes bad, it will ruin your credit as well as the person you co-sign for and will hurt the relationship in the process. The primary warning sign: If they had good credit, they wouldn't need you!

Usury is the lending of money with an interest charge for its use—especially the lending of money at exorbitant rates. Think of those sub-prime credit cards, payday loans or unsecured loans that charge high interest, frequently over thirty percent. In Proverbs 28:8, the Lord tells us that *"Whoever increases wealth by taking interest or profit from the poor amasses it for another, who will be kind to the poor."*

Lending refers to loaning money out to others for temporary use on the condition of repayment with interest. In Deuteronomy 15:8 (NASB), we are told: *"You shall freely open your hand to him and shall generously lend him sufficient for his need in whatever he lacks."* Psalm 112:5 (NASB) reminds us: *"It is well with a man who is gracious and lends."* Nehemiah 5:10 (NLT) goes further: *"We have been lending money and grain to the people, but let's stop this charging interest."*

In the Old Testament, debt was a form of slavery. There were provisions in the Law that every seven years, Israelis were supposed to be released from their debt and every fifty years, during the year of Jubilee, they were also to be forgiven the debt. However, there is no Biblical record they ever actually celebrated a year of Jubilee.

They were also not to charge interest to fellow Hebrews, but they could charge the Gentiles. One of my Jewish friends told me God created Gentiles so someone could pay interest! To be a lender is a blessing, to be a borrower is a curse or at least an indication you are in hard times.

In Nehemiah's time, having a mortgage on your property was a sign of desperation. Things have sure changed over the centuries. Nowadays, it's rare to hear of someone actually paying cash for a home. Did you know the word "mortgage" is actually mort (death) and gage (grip)! Mortgage literally means "death-grip."

The most direct passage on debt in the New Testament is in Romans.

Romans 13:8 (NKJV)
Owe no one anything except to love one another, for he who loves another has fulfilled the law.

Some argue that this doesn't really apply to financial debt. But if you refer to Chapter 13 in context, Paul is clearly talking about submitting to governing authorities and owing taxes.

In Jesus' day, just as today, debt was a hot topic. Many of His parables and teachings touched on the subject of finances and debt. It wasn't unusual for people to be indentured or put in debtors' prison or sold as slaves if they were unable to pay their debt. For many, there was no way out of debt.

Jesus has a unique perspective on debt. He frequently ties it to the forgiveness of sin. Just as there was no way out of debt, there was no way out of sin except through Him. Just as they couldn't pay their debt, they couldn't pay their way out of sin.

Our Lord also counseled us not to turn away from someone who wants to borrow if we can help (Matthew 5:42, NLT). And He encourages us to forgive our debts as others, including Him, forgive us. In other words, be generous as He has been generous to us.

To summarize, the Bible clearly teaches that borrowing is to be discouraged, but it is not forbidden or called sin. (It would make a stewardship pastor's job easier if it was, but I digress). Lending is a blessing, but borrowing places us in a master/servant role with a creditor. At a bare minimum, according to Scripture, debt should be used in an ultra-conservative manner.

The first time I borrowed money from my Dad, our relationship underwent a fundamental change to this master/servant arrangement, which was very uncomfortable for both of us. It felt awkward to call home and talk about any kind of money I used for something other than paying him back. I wanted to pay him back quickly and get our relationship on its correct footing. And I did.

Under the Biblical plan, our goal is to get completely out of debt. This will take time, planning, and careful stewardship and management of our money. The ideal position is to have no debt and also have significant financial margin to be flexible to follow the Holy Spirit.

I encourage you not to develop your theology about debt from one verse—or even one man's teaching. Take a full view of the Scriptures to form your own view on the subject. As I said in an earlier chapter, I don't want to talk you into it, I want you to discover for yourself in the Word of God so being debt-free becomes a personal conviction.

Early in my position as a pastor, a young man I counseled wanted desperately to go into the mission field. He had a heart for missions and a zeal for the Lord. He also had over $100,000 in student loans. The Mission Board turned him down because there was no way he could go into the mission field and afford the debt burden. He was heartbroken—he couldn't fulfill his calling because of debt.

There is a definite connection between debt and your calling. When Missy and I were looking for me to go into full-time ministry, we knew the Lord had called us to get completely out of debt before that happened. Using the Debt Snowball, we paid off $88,000, which was everything but the house. The month I made the last payment on the snowball is when I got the call for the interview for my first full-time ministry position.

> There is a definite connection between debt and your calling.

The new position called for a significant pay cut. I wouldn't have been able to take the position if we were still in debt. We couldn't have afforded it. Due to being debt-free, we rearranged our lifestyle and answered the call to full-time ministry.

WHERE DO AMERICANS STAND ON DEBT?

Unfortunately, not on very solid ground. Here are some numbers that boggled my mind when I first saw them in *Moneyzine*[1] and *Hoffman Brinker*[2].

In 2010, the total consumer debt stood at $2.4 **trillion**! That's an average of $7,800 debt for every man, woman and child. Thirty-three percent of that is revolving debt such as credit cards. This means it just cycles and recycles every month. Actually, it acts more like a spiral, always going up. The other sixty-seven percent is in loans such as car loans, student loans and mortgages.

Amazing to me, in 2005, $33.2 billion dollars' worth of fast food was charged. In 2006, it jumped to $51 billion, an increase of nearly fifty-four percent. We, as Americans, are rapidly increasing our debt to buy food. And it's not even basic groceries. It's Big Macs and Whoppers.

Credit cards seem to be taking over the world. Statistics show the average consumer has four credit cards. Ten percent have more than ten cards. The average household carries an average of $6,500 in credit card debt from month to month.

When I teach this chapter to classes in churches, we end it with having a ceremony where we cut up our credit cards. One couple had over sixty credit cards! I talked with them later, and he told me he saw himself as a success because all those cards showed him that someone saw him as valuable and worthy. Until that night, his goal had been to get as many credit cards as possible. Now, his worth is focused on his relationships with his family and God, not

---

[1] *money-zine.com/financial-planning/debt-consolidation/consumer-debt-statistics/*
[2] *hoffmanbrinker.com/credit-card-debt-statistics.html*

how much plastic he carries.

Another counselee came to me eaten up with stress and nerves around her finances. She had fallen into the pattern of using one credit card to pay off another. She had accumulated $110,000 of credit card debt, and she had no way to pay it off. She couldn't keep floating the debt because all her cards were maxed out. Now the creditors were calling. She handled all the finances in the home. Her husband didn't know anything about what was going on in their finances, and she was scared to tell him. I called them into my office and, together, we explained the situation. He freaked out and was really upset. Could you blame him?

Then I told him it was his fault. He was not really happy to hear that either, but he listened. By leaving all the finances in her hands, he had abdicated his mantle of leadership in the family. He hadn't managed his household and put his wife under undue stress to where she couldn't even talk to him about it. Although he did not handle the day-to-day money management, he should have been knowledgeable of their financial position.

He was brokenhearted, and they prayed and repented. They took financial classes and other counseling and programs we offered through the church. Eventually, they did have to file bankruptcy but rebuilt their lives and family on Christian principles. The last time I saw them, they were walking through church holding hands. Previously, she would walk six feet behind him.

As a nation, we don't appear to be in much better shape. The total U.S. Government debt is $16 trillion! It took our country 200 years to reach one trillion in debt. In just thirty-seven years, we've added another $15 trillion. And it's not just one party doing it. President Reagan added $1.4 trillion of debt in his eight years. President George W. Bush added $3.3 trillion over eight years. President Obama added $5.1 trillion in his first four years. This irresponsibility cannot continue.

I am not making a political statement, simple mathematics say it cannot continue. The country needs to wake up and elect responsible leaders on both sides of the aisle who will govern as good stewards.

How much is a Trillion Dollars?

One hundred $100s = $10,000

$1 million (100 packets of $10,000

$100 Million fits on a pallet

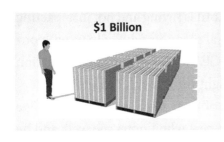

$1 Billion

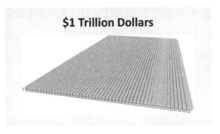

$1 Trillion Dollars

MY PHILOSOPHY ABOUT DEBT AND FINANCES

As you can no doubt tell, the whole idea of debt and managing our finances is very real and personal for me.

My goal is to be debt-free—mortgage and all, as the Lord blesses.

Missy and I are striving to live out a plan where we save one-third of our money, give away one-third and live on one-third. This is requiring some serious discipline and lifestyle adjustments, but we believe it is achievable.

We don't use unsecured loans or credit cards as part of our personal budget. I'm not saying credit cards are a sin—although they may be to some people if they're used in the wrong way. This is something each of us has to wrestle out for ourselves, but I'm a firm advocate of not using credit cards. They open the door to all kinds of problems and temptation we don't need.

We will never co-sign a loan for anyone else. To do so violates Biblical teaching.

By saving aggressively, we'll be able to guard and increase our margin to be in a position to respond to God's leading to do something as soon as He says to do it.

Any major financial decisions we make, such as cars, homes and college for our kids, will be done with a multitude of counselors. Obviously, Missy and I have to come into agreement about the decision. But, in specific areas, we will also talk with other people we trust.

There are spiritual counselors and leaders we talk with to make sure we're understanding what the Lord is saying and not just reacting to last night's pizza. We have financial planners who help us with our long-range goals. We work with our CPA to stay on top of our situation and to make sure we're doing the right things with our money.

I think it's pretty clear I'm a bit of a car freak, so before I plunge into buying a car, I talk with a car expert who knows me well, and he knows my tendencies about buying and selling cars. We have a strong relationship, so he won't hesitate to tell me if I'm doing something stupid.

In the same way, we have a home expert who loves us enough to speak straight about our thinking regarding buying a new home or remodeling what we have.

Proverbs 11:14 (NKJV)
Where there is no counsel, the people fall; but in the multitude of counselors there is safety.

If I'm embarrassed to tell someone what I'm doing financially—then I probably shouldn't be doing it. Missy and I live with financial accountability from multiple angles.

Each relationship has taken time to develop, but we prayed for a group of godly counselors. Then I wrote a list of financial fields I wanted to develop relationships in to give me wisdom at decision crossroads.

> If I'm embarrassed to tell someone what I'm doing financially—then I probably shouldn't be doing it.

1. Prayer Team

We asked a couple of families if they would pray for us. I send them ministry updates and ask for prayer feedback. They cover any and everything in our life with prayer. We stay in close relationship over a monthly dinner and randomly-timed phone calls throughout the month.

2. Financial Advisor

We use a financial planner who is similar in age but has a lot of industry experience. We set goals together, and he holds us accountable to our goals.

3. Certified Public Accountant

I could do our taxes, but if I did, I would miss out on the wisdom of our CPA. He not only helps with our taxes, he is a key counselor on financial goals.

4. Car Counselor

Every time I get the car bug or need to make a car decision, I process the decision with my car guru friend who happens to be in the car business. Even if I do not buy a car through him, I still process with him. When I have made car decisions without his input, it has cost me money!

5. Home Counselor

I don't make many home decisions, but I have found a friend who is really sharp on real estate. He can help me with area, timing, rates and whether or not to upgrade items. It is his area of expertise, and he always gives me angles to think about that I had not previously considered. He also is a good enough friend to tell me I am about to make a bad decision.

Make your own list of financial counselors and pray for wise counselors. You may have different needs than we do, and our lists will also change as life seasons change. I don't need a retirement expert to help me preserve the retirement nest egg—yet. I no longer own a business, so my need for business counsel is limited; however, you may need these counselors the most.

SOME COMMON FORMS OF DEBT

Debt comes in many forms, and every time we sign up for a debt, we're signing to be a slave to whoever holds the note, whether it's a bank, a credit union, a friend or a family member. We are entering into an unequal relationship because that institution or person now holds power over our money and us. If you do not believe me, just miss a few payments, and you will feel the puppet master pull the strings.

Pay Day Loans are short-term, unsecured loans that charge super high interest. While they seem inexpensive at the start, the annual interest rate can be over 300%. Understandably, there is a very high default rate with these loans, and it is extremely hard to get out of this debt. You either have to get a large cash influx or squeeze your monthly budget to get out of the loan. You may have to get a second job just to gain enough momentum to pay off the loan. Either way, these are tough to pay off. Better to not enter in from the start.

Read on to see examples of the charges and annual percentage rates (APR) that popular Texas lenders charge for a two-week loan period.[3]

	Amt Borrowed	APR	Finance Charges
Pay Day One			
	$100	598.51%	$22.88
	$200	596.64%	$45.77
	$500	596.62%	$114.42
	$1000	596.62%	$225.24
Cash Net U.S.A			
	$100	664.29%	$25.48
	$200	664.29%	$50.96
	$500	664.29%	$127.60
	$1000	664.29%	$254.79
NCP Finance Limited Partnership			
	$100	641.59%	$25.38
	$200	641.59%	$50.75
	$500	651.79%	$126.91
	$1000	681.77%	$253.83
Midwest R&S Corporation			
	$100	583.45%	$22.38
	$200	583.45%	$44.74
	$500	583.45%	$111.91
	$1000	583.45%	$223.43

---

[3]*paydayloansonlineresource.org/average-interest-rates-for-payday-loans*

Credit cards with their 90-day, no interest teasers or balance transfers, lead to impulse buying. Studies by Dunn and Bradstreet and McDonald's[4] have shown that people who use plastic frequently purchased more than those who used cash. It just feels easier to throw an extra burger or dessert in the bag because we're not forking over real money—yet!

Recently, Missy and I took a trip to New Mexico. We took $250 in cash for meals and entertainment. We came home with $60 because we managed vacation cash differently than a credit card. It was cash— we could see it leave the wallet and not come back. Cash is harder to spend, and because we had cash, we made wiser decisions and had a real good time.

Eighty-four percent of college students have credit cards, according to a Sallie Mae study[5], even though most of them have not established any credit history. They have little income, so they rapidly max their cards out and run up fees that keep them tied to the credit card company for years. Eighty-four percent of undergraduates had at least one credit card, up from 76 percent in 2004. On average, students have 4.6 credit cards, and half of college students had four or more cards. The average (mean) balance grew to $3,173, higher than any of the previous studies. Median debt grew from 2004's $946 to $1,645.

Credit card debt is a touchy subject. I read a study recently that said discussing credit card debt is at the top of the list of things people won't talk about (right up there with details of your love life). This is one reason credit card debt is such a burden. People privately carry the emotional and spiritual weight of that debt.

And, despite recent efforts to control the credit card companies, their collection practices are awful: repeated and harassing phone calls, threatening letters, all types of coercion to get as much money out of you as possible. I recently met with a family where the mother

---

[4]*hoffmanbrinker.com/credit-card-debt-statistics.html*
[5]*salliemae.com/about/news_info/newsreleases/041309.aspx*

was dying. She was in the last days of her life and yet, as her daughters were dealing with this intensely emotional and personal crisis, a credit card company was calling and getting ugly, trying to manipulate the children into giving them some of Mom's money in the midst of releasing her to heaven.

Home loans or **mortgages** have a Latin root to them. Remember, it means "death-grip." Think about that. Someone has a death grip on your finances. I recommend people take out fifteen-year mortgages or shorter. The longer your mortgage, the more you pay in interest, and the more likely you are to give the holder more money than you actually paid for the house. Add the mortgage to your Debt Snowball, but make sure to build up your savings before you start the ball rolling. I've worked with several families who actually over-focused on paying off the mortgage. When they lost their jobs, they didn't have enough in their savings or emergency fund to float them along until they got their next job. Many went into foreclosure or sold their house short as a result.

Home equity loans and **home equity lines of credit** tap into the equity in your house—the difference between what you owe on your house and what you can sell it for to provide a source of cash. It's actually credit, and it's based on the assumption your house will continue to increase in value. Well, the last few years have shown that's not a dependable premise. Banks pushed these loans, and people misused their house like never-ending piggy banks. One bank told me I would never have to worry about balancing my checkbook because I could just tap into my line of credit if I came up short. Unfortunately, even if you're up to date on your first mortgage, lenders can still take you into foreclosure if you fall behind on these lines of credit.

When I teach these principles to a group that includes business leaders, someone will inevitably say you can't run a business without **business debt**. I disagree. I *know* you can run a business without debt because I did it with my construction business in Florida. Just like you plan your family's finances, you plan your business finances. It takes a lot of work and diligence, but it can be done—especially with the business tools available today. Here are some debt-free companies operating today:

T Rowe Price

Bed, Bath and Beyond

Amazon

Apple

MasterCard *(which is kind of ironic considering their business model is based on your debt)*

A few years back, Walgreen's and Eckerd's drug stores were in heavy competition. They were building on opposite corners from each other, competing ferociously for your business. There was one major difference between them—Walgreen's was debt-free. They had the margin to sustain the battle. Eckerd's was loaded with debt and didn't have the ability to keep up with competition and eventually collapsed and was sold to CVS.

Church debt can be financially, emotionally and spiritually burdensome. It can lead to strife and division within a congregation. Many churches seem to have the philosophy of "If we build it, they will come." This is not always true because the need to build isn't really there. It's a misperception that new buildings and expansion will draw people in. My counsel is to build only when you have actual growth problems. Wait until you have run out of room, get creative, then build. And be very conservative with construction and add a plan from the beginning to get out of debt. Borrowing should be limited to one percent of your annual revenue. Gateway Church is working toward its goal of being completely debt-free. Even though we have borrowed to manage growth, we have secured a short-term loan (10 years vs the industry average of 20–25), and our debt service amount is under 10% of our yearly budget. That's pretty conservative.

I am not a fan of **student loans**. Recent history shows how expensive and burdensome they are. Some students are graduating with more than $100,000 student loan debt and entering a job market with few prospects to be able to earn enough to pay it off. Student loans are very hard to pay off. And the school loan lenders can garnish up to fifteen percent of your wages.

If you absolutely have to go to college to pursue your career goals, find a way to work through college and not take any debt. Consider working for a year or two to save money. Believe me, the life experience of working, of putting your own skin in the game to pursue your dream, is way more valuable than paying off the debt.

If you have student loans, live like you did when you were in school—as frugally as possible—and then pay off the debt using a Debt Snowball.

> Student loans are very hard to pay off.

When I graduated from high school, I had some partial scholarship opportunities, but not enough to cover the full cost. Even at that age, I did not feel comfortable taking on the debt of a student loan. So I didn't take on any loans and only took one class. Instead, I started a business and was making a good living. Life kind of derailed the college dream, but I always knew that someday I'd have the chance. In the meantime, God trained me to do what I'm doing now. About two years ago, my faithfulness was rewarded when the Elders of Gateway offered to bless me if I wanted to go back to college. So God has made a way for me to get my education, in part because of my faithfulness and obedience to His call.

Avoid **family loans** at all costs. And I do mean *all*. They usually turn into a disaster and can severely strain, if not destroy, family relationships. No amount of money is worth years of estrangement and bitterness. Scripture says the borrower is the slave to the lender, and do you really want Grandma to be the master of *your* universe?

Another harsh master is the **IRS**. If they say you owe them money, you are guilty until proven innocent, and you're probably in for a long, hard battle. The government can garnish wages and take property to pay the debt. So keep your records and pay your taxes accurately.

The Bible tells us we have a clear responsibility to pay our debts. If we don't, we are wicked. (Psalm 37:21).

For many, bankruptcy seems to provide a way out of financial turmoil, but it is no longer the panacea it once was. The laws have been updated, and it is very difficult to successfully file for personal bankruptcy (commonly referred to as Chapter 7). There is now a means test you must meet. If you make over a certain pre-set amount, you will be given a repayment plan. And you will still be responsible for spousal and child support, some taxes and student loans. It no longer rids you of all debt.

A Chapter 13 bankruptcy is actually a debt reorganization process. The debt is not abolished. It is restructured to satisfy your creditors.

A Chapter 11 bankruptcy is a reorganization of business debt.

Our bankruptcy laws have their origin in the Biblical principles of the sabbatical year and the year of Jubilee. I have had feedback from many who have taken that path, that bankruptcy is almost as tough as a divorce.

PRACTICAL APPLICATIONS

Questions to Consider

Before you make any decisions about taking on debt, there are four questions you need to ask yourself. These are four areas to discuss with your spouse and your accountability partners. If you're single, I urge you to develop a relationship with someone you feel very comfortable with in discussing your finances. These are not decisions you should make alone.

1. The Tomorrow Test

James 4:13–16 (NLT)
Look here, you who say, "Today or tomorrow we are going to a certain town and will stay there a year. We will do business there and make a profit." How do you know what your life will be like tomorrow? Your life is like the morning fog—it's here a little while, then it's gone. What you ought to say is, "If the Lord wants us to, we will live and do this or that." Otherwise you are boasting about your own plans, and all such boasting is evil.

The Tomorrow Test asks the questions:

- *If my income is cut next year, can I still pay this loan off on schedule?*
- *If I lost my job and had to take another job making a lot less, could I still afford this loan?*
- *Am I making this decision based on a hope of future income, no matter how secure or insecure it might be?*

Never take a loan expecting any kind of financial increase. You will fail the Tomorrow Test.

2. The Security Test

- *If I have to sell the asset, will it be enough to cover what I owe on it?*
- *Do I have equity in the asset?*

In other words, the loan must be much less than the value of whatever item I purchased.

3. The Freedom Test

- *Does this loan restrict my freedom or limit me in any way? Does it hinder my financial, emotional or spiritual freedom?*
- *Does it limit my ability to give, to change jobs or to move in any way God directs? Many times, God is trying to get us to slow down so He can show an option that doesn't involve going into debt. We need to wait, be patient and hear what He has to say to us.*
- *Does this debt build or hurt my testimony? Does it show God shining forth in my life?*

4. The Dependence Test

- *By taking this debt, am I forcing myself into a position of being dependent on others?*
- *Who am I depending on: man or God?*
- *Am I going around God's already provided provision?*
- *Am I willing to wait on Him or must I have it now?*

I've counseled with people who did take the time to answer these four simple tests. Only the Lord can take care of many of these loans. Before we take on debt, we need to take a step back and look at the reality of where we are today. And then we have to prayerfully make a plan.

HOW DO WE BREAK THE DEBT CYCLE?

First, we give. Giving changes our hearts. It injects the Lord's provision into our lives.

Second, we need to change our spending habits and determine to live on less than we earn so we can create a financial margin. We live on a *written* budget, and we avoid magazines, television shows and websites that fuel our desires to make purchases. I easily get the car bug and want to start shopping for another car. When this happens, I've learned to stay away from auto magazines and websites about cars because I know I will talk myself into buying a car before my finances are ready.

> Giving changes our hearts. It injects the Lord's provision into our lives.

Third, we commit to no additional debt. The credit cards get cut up. We're not going into debt for anything else. As we keep making payments, eventually we will get out, and we can add all that money we've been paying out to increasing our margin and our giving.

Fourth, communicate honestly and frequently with our spouse and accountability partner. Get to know each other's spending patterns and talk openly about them—nicely. Don't impulse buy. Commit to calling each other before making a purchase over a certain amount. For Missy and I, it's thirty dollars.

And don't buy on emotion.

One day, I realized that while I love to buy and sell cars, I couldn't stay content with a car for very long. I approached an elder in the church, and we prayed about it. I asked God if there was a reason I struggle with contentment when it came to cars. The elder told me God had shown him it had something to do with a red sports car and an experience I had in high school.

And it came back to me. I had a friend who had a red sports car, and she would let me borrow it during the last period of the day. I would have a blast joyriding around town and always returning it to her at the end of the school day.

One day, we ended up in a very ugly conversation and she said, "At least my parents can afford to send me to this private school." That stung because my parents struggled to make my tuition, and we also received financial aid from the school.

I made a vow to always be self-sufficient and to always drive a very nice car. I was viewing my self-worth by what I drove, instead of what God had put in me.

Once I confessed and dealt with the issue, I've been much more content with my cars.

There may be deeper issues with your debt patterns—issues you need to explore with your spouse or pastoral staff.

Fifth, create a Debt Snowball. List your debts from smallest to largest. Make minimum payments on the larger ones as you attack the smallest debt first. Sell things. Pull money from your budget, and throw it on the smallest debt. When you've paid off the first one, take that payment and add it to the next debt. Keep doing it until all the debt is paid off.

> In your budget, every dollar has a name and a purpose.

Finally, *save, save, save*—as much as you can, whenever you can. Remember, in your budget, every dollar has a name and a purpose. Name some of it *savings.*

Getting out of debt takes patience, planning and diligence. You didn't get into debt overnight, so don't expect to get out of it overnight either. But commit to doing it. Apply the principles we've taught in this chapter and this book, and it will happen.

And you will find that you love paying cash for things.

CHAPTER EIGHT

LIFE STEWARDSHIP

What do I mean by Life Stewardship? Life stewardship is living out God's calling on my life. He didn't place us here to scurry meaninglessly through life like mice in a maze. He has a plan for each of us, for our own lives, and for showing Him to others, to draw them closer to Him.

How do I figure out God's calling in my life? If I don't know where I'm headed, if I don't know how God wired me, why get out of debt? Why get our finances in order just to reach a box canyon of not knowing why we've done this?

Sometimes we may think, *"I'm doing well financially, but I'm not sure about my calling."* We find ourselves saying, "I don't know why I'm here. I don't know what God wants me to do. Does He even have a specific plan for my life?"

The answer is, "Yes, He does."

"Well, Pastor Gunnar, how do I figure out what it is?"

I'm so glad you asked.

Many times, finding our calling feels like we're flying in the dark.

When I was eighteen-years-old, I took flying lessons. And it was fun hopping around in little Cessnas—until I had to fly at night over the ocean! That was eerie and downright scary. The lighting in the plane is dim, and it's hard to find the horizon. If the moon is shining, its reflection off the water creates distraction and confusion, which is a dangerous thing to deal with in a plane. It messes with your head, and you can't tell which direction is up. One moon is in the sky, the other's in the water. And it's hard to tell which one is the real one. You aim for one moon, and you could be heading for the water.

The only way to survive is to rely on the gauges in the plane—on the altimeter and the other instruments that tell me exactly where I am. I have to trust them. I have to have faith that the gauges work and that they're accurate.

It's the same in life. The direction may feel right, but we're headed toward the water. Just like relying on the instruments to fly, in life we have to rely on our instruments—our relationship with God and His Word.

When seeking His calling on our life, it's far more important to discover who we *are* over what we *do*. What we *do* is the outflow of who we *are*. Who we *are* in life needs to be channeled through God-given gifts into what we *do*. Another way to look at it is: Once we figure out who we are, our natural God-given gifts are developed into skills to serve Him and help others.

> In life we have to rely on our instruments—our relationship with God and His Word.

INSIGHTS INTO DEVELOPING YOUR LIFE STEWARDSHIP

There are a few insights I've learned that I think are very helpful in identifying your calling and living your life of stewardship.

Identity – Who Are You in Christ?
This depends on one question: Do you know Christ? If you do, your identity is spectacular. If you don't know Him, then you're in trouble. Let's see what Scripture tells us.

2 Corinthians 5:17 (ESV)
Therefore, if anyone is in Christ, he is a new creation. The old has passed away; behold, the new has come.

Romans 8:1 (ESV)
There is therefore now no condemnation for those who are in Christ Jesus.

1 Peter 2:9 (ESV)
But you are a chosen race, a royal priesthood, a holy nation, a people for his own possession, that you may proclaim the excellencies of him who called you out of darkness into his marvelous light.

Romans 12:2 (ESV)
Do not be conformed to this world, but be transformed by the renewal of your mind, that by testing you may discern what is the will of God, what is good and acceptable and perfect.

John 1:12 (ESV)
But to all who did receive him, who believed in his name, he gave the right to become children of God.

2 Corinthians 5:21 (ESV)
For our sake he made him to be sin who knew no sin, so that in him we might become the righteousness of God.

When we bundle these passages as a group, we get a glimpse of *WHO* we are in Christ: New creation, transformed mind, royal priesthood, child of God, in Christ the righteousness of God.

Because of the work Jesus accomplished on the cross, each and every one of us has a MASSIVE calling from God.

This identity will get us out of bed in the morning feeling pretty good about ourselves, pretty spectacular—all made possible by knowing Jesus' work on the cross.

> Because of the work Jesus accomplished on the cross, each and every one of us has a MASSIVE calling from God.

We're amazingly gifted, called by Christ, worthy of His sacrifice.

We have a Bible full of words of affirmation of who we are in Christ.

Gifting

Gifting is the second area in this life of stewardship I want to explore with you.

Ephesians 2:10 (NKJV) tells us, *"For we are His workmanship, created in Christ Jesus for good works, which God prepared beforehand so that we should walk in them." (emphasis added)*

How do I know what works I was created to do? What are my gifts? I need to become a student of myself and of God's Word. I need to figure out what makes me tick, how I'm wired.

We've all heard, "Love God as you love yourself." The problem is people don't know how to love themselves, so they don't know how to love God.

Here are some tools for helping discover who we are and what our gifts are.

One is to find our strengths. Management and leadership guru, Peter Drucker, once wrote: "Most people think they know what they are good at. They are usually wrong. And yet, a person can only perform from strengths."

Did you ever meet someone who thinks they're really good at a sport like basketball or tennis or golf? You play with them and find out they're really awful. This is what Drucker is talking about.

A few years ago, scientists tested freshmen who were entering a couple of prestigious colleges. They found basically two groups of students. What separated them was how fast they read. One read at 90 words per minute. The other read at 270. The scientists knew students needed to be able to read quickly if they were going to make it in college. They put all the students through six weeks of speed reading classes. The theory was the students in the 90-word-per-minute group would catch up to the 270 group.

They at first thought their experiment was a success. The 90-word-per-minute group did improve—but to nearly 300 words per minute!

Then they re-tested the 270 group. Their scores soared to *2,790 words per minute!* Furthermore, research found this group was naturally inclined to read fast. They had a natural gift for it.

Leadership studies used to preach: "Find your weaknesses and work on them; improve them." The problem with this approach is, if you're not good at math, you're probably never going to get real good at math no matter what you do. And you'll end up frustrated.

Along the same lines, if you're a natural athlete and train yourself, you're going to get much faster and stronger because you're genetically inclined to do it.

It's the same thing with everything else in life. Whatever you're good at, you have the ability to rapidly advance and be even better. Your weaknesses are what they are, and they're not likely to improve a whole lot.

At *gallupstrengthcenter.com*, you'll find a self-assessment you can take for around $10. The results are a profile identifying your five greatest strengths plus action points and guides for understanding the results.

Dr. Donald Clifton created StrengthsFinder, an online personal assessment test based on his lifelong research which outlines your personal strengths. It advocates focusing on building strengths rather than focusing on weaknesses. They have distilled the theory into practice by interviewing 1.7 million professionals from varying fields, have quantified the different "Personal Themes" of the subjects and have come up with 34 distinct attributes (*strengthsfinder.com*).

My StrengthsFinder Profile identified my strongest areas as:

WOO – This stands for Winning People Over. I have the ability to win you over to my side of an argument or discussion, and you will like me.

Learner – I'm going to study things that interest me, even if they're not related to each other. I'm naturally curious and want to learn.

Communicator – I can tell you what I learned in a way that makes sense.

Futuristic – I'm a forward thinker. I'm also a bit of a daydreamer, looking forward to future possibilities.

Arranger – I love to help put people in places where they will do really well.

I'm also a bit of a smart aleck, although it's not an official StrengthsFinder standard. One time, I started selling cookies during executive team meetings, and I made a profit at it.

Another tool for discovering your giftings is the DiSC Personality Profile (*thediscpersonalitytest.com*). This tool helps you learn how you are wired. It focuses on your personality, not your strengths.

DiSC stands for:

Dominance or **D**rive, which relates to control, power and assertiveness.
Inducement or **I**nfluence, which relates to social situations and communications.
Submission or **S**teadiness, which relates to patience, persistence and thoughtfulness.
Compliance, **C**aution or **C**onscientiousness, which relates to structure and organization.

If you can figure out how you're wired, you can gravitate toward your strengths. This is life-giving. You can rapidly move forward in your development without getting frustrated trying to work on your weaknesses, which, at best, will only improve marginally.

If you're a leader and oversee staff, you can figure out their strengths and weaknesses. You can tailor their jobs and roles so they can quickly develop their skill sets and advance as their strengths grow. You end up with happy employees who are highly effective and efficient. They're having a great time working in their strength sets.

Unfortunately, for most of us, it's a different story.

At the end of high school, people start asking: "What would you like to do when you graduate?" The answer usually is something along the lines of: "Be rich—whatever will make me a lot of money; maybe being a doctor." But you don't have empathy, you don't like dealing with medicine, and you really don't like the sight of blood. You end up in a place where you don't fit.

Or we follow in Dad's footprints. *"He's a CPA, so I'll be a CPA—*

> If you can figure out how you're wired, you can gravitate toward your strengths.

but I'm not naturally gifted in this area, and I hate numbers." School becomes a grind.

You get out of college, and instead of doing something you really love, you do something you've been trained to do because you (or your parents) poured all this money into your education, and you don't want to disappoint yourself or your parents.

You go into a career you don't really like, get married, have kids. Now you have financial responsibilities. You stay in the job you don't like, that you're not wired for, because you need the income. And you're not excelling in the job.

Next thing you know, you're forty years old, and you think, *"I'm not happy in life."*

You come to Gateway (or a church like it), and you sit under the teaching, attend the classes and you learn: *Oh, I'm not happy because I'm doing something I'm not naturally wired for.*

Then the stewardship pastor starts asking questions and working with you to figure out how you are gifted and wired and called by God. You begin to discover what you're supposed to be doing, and life starts to be a lot more fun.

Gateway has over 5,000 volunteers and we use the StrengthsFinder test to find their giftings. Then we match people with the areas of service that best utilize their gifts. When they come to church, they have a lot of fun serving.

Another tool for learning your strengths and giftings, especially in your personal life, is to take the Five Love Languages Assessment (*5lovelanguages.com*). This is a great marriage communication tool because it helps you to see how you and your spouse interact with each other.

Here are my Love Language scores:

10   Physical Touch

8   Words of Affirmation

5	Receiving Gifts
4	Quality Time
3	Acts of Service

My wife's are about 180 degrees opposite from mine. If I try to communicate from my primary love language, and hers is different, she's not going to understand what I'm doing. We'll have tension and friction.

When she and I put our StrengthsFinder, DiSC and Love Language scores together, we found our arguments were in areas where our strengths didn't line up.

For example, her number one strength is Belief. When my number one meets her number one, she feels like I'm trying to manipulate her and talk her into something. I feel like she's stubborn.

When I bring her a gift, I think she's going to think I'm buttering her up. Actually, she thinks I'm wonderful because her number one Love Language is receiving gifts.

Mine is physical touch. If I approach her with physical touch, it can lead to miscommunication.

We can use our StrengthsFinder, DiSC and our Love Languages to discover why things didn't work out on the job or at home as smoothly as we thought they would.

Timing

Timing is the third area of discovering your calling in life stewardship. If we get all the other areas right but miss the timing, we can make a mess.

Let's look at some Biblical examples of timing.

When Joseph was a youth, he had a vision of his older siblings bowing down to him. In his immaturity, he brags about this to his family. When he's thirty years old, he enters Pharaoh's service. When he bragged about his vision, I'm sure he would never have planned his path the way it happened: Sold into slavery, became Potiphar's assistant only to be falsely accused by his adulterous wife, followed by prison, then high pressure dream interpretations led to his promotion. In God's timing, He couldn't promote Joseph until he had matured.

When Moses was a young man, he burned with a desire to free his people. But when he defended a fellow Israelite from an Egyptian, by killing the Egyptian, his people wouldn't follow him. Exodus 2:14 conveys the response he received: *"The man said, 'Who made you ruler and judge over us? Are you thinking of killing me as you killed the Egyptian?'"* You could say his people stayed away by the thousands. When Pharaoh tried to kill him, he fled into the wilderness. Forty years later, he encountered God in a burning bush. God sent him back to Egypt to free the Israelites in a miraculous way. Now the time was right.

Even Jesus had to wait for His Father's timing. Look at Jesus' first recorded miracle:

John 2:3–4
When the wine was gone, Jesus' mother said to him, "They have no more wine." "Woman, why do you involve me?" Jesus replied. "My hour has not yet come."

Someday, Jesus will be back to rule on earth. But because of His love and great mercy for those who don't know Him, the time for His return has not yet come.

Timing in life is critical. When we lived in Florida, I wanted to be on the staff at my small church more than anything. I volunteered; I served; I made myself available in any way I could. It didn't happen because it was not God's plan. But He used that time to train and prepare me. At about the same time, God was launching a church in

Southlake, Texas, through Pastor Robert Morris that would fit me like a glove. I needed time to develop and so did Gateway Church. When the time was right, He brought us together.

As a wise pastor once said, "If you're going to miss God's timing, it's always better to be behind Him than ahead of Him."

Preparation – Developing Our Skills

We've figured out our identity and our gifting, and we're waiting on God's timing. Now, what do we do? This is when we prepare for the intersection of life opportunities—that time when we hear God's call and recognize the part we are to play.

If you haven't figured it out by now, getting our finances in order is only a means to an end. It frees us to make life changes when God calls. We are open and free to answer what God has prepared for us.

As you read this, you can't see from the beginning to the end. We don't know what opportunities are in the future, either tomorrow, next year or twenty years from now.

But this is not a time of simply waiting. This is a time of preparing—of getting ourselves in the position to respond to God's call. We don't want to be in the position of those in the Bible who wanted to first go bury their dead or check out their new oxen. We prepare so we can move when God tells us to.

How do we figure this out? How do we prepare?

The Bible tells us how:

Psalm 119:105 (KJV)
Thy word is a lamp unto my feet, and a light unto my path.

This doesn't say the Word is a high beam or a spotlight, it's a lamp. When we walk with a lamp in the darkness, we really only see what's right in front of us. So, how do we begin to prepare for the opportunities God has for us?

Personal Retreat Days are like a sabbatical. Periodically, take some time by yourself. It can be an afternoon, a full day or even a week. But take at least one afternoon a month.

Every member of our ministry team participates in this practice. It has proven to be very effective, not only for the individual staff, but the ministry team and the whole church benefits as well.

Grab your Bible and journal or notebook. Turn off your cell phone or leave it at home. You want to get rid of all possible distractions during this time. Find someplace quiet like a park or a beach. Maybe drive to a secluded spot and sit in your car.

You want a place where it's just you and God. Ask the Lord: "What are You doing in my life right now? Am I being prepared for something? What are You saying to me? Are You speaking change or are You speaking stay steady?"

Pray, read the Word, and write down what you hear the Lord say.

When I take my personal retreat day, I pray about my relationship with Him. I pray through questions such as: "Lord, how am I doing? Is there something in my heart I need to change? Are You speaking to me but I haven't caught it yet?" He usually has a few things to say to me too. And He's grateful for our undivided attention.

Then, I pray about my family, both immediate and extended. He will frequently give me insight into one of my family members, showing me things they're going through that I didn't see.

I pray for the church and the stewardship ministry. Almost every new initiative of the stewardship team at Gateway has come out of someone's personal retreat time.

You can apply this to your business as well. The CEO of ServiceMaster's, a group of companies like Merry Maid, Terminix, TruGreen and others that provide a variety of services to individuals and businesses, would pray for God to show him what companies to start and acquire. The walls of his conference room display plaques for each of these God-inspired companies.

In terms of your business, your ministry and your calling, why not turn to God—the ruler of the world—whose eyes roam to and fro, seeking who is faithful (2 Chronicles 16:9).

> Almost every new initiative of the stewardship team at Gateway has come out of someone's personal retreat time.

I also pray about my leadership, asking where I need to grow and change. "Am I efficient? What technologies should I be using? What do You want me to do with my schedule and upcoming opportunities so my time and talents best serve You, my church, my team and my family? What do I need to know about my team members? How can I help them grow and prepare for the next steps You have for them? Are there ideas You want me to bring to my church leadership?"

I'm ADD and easily distracted. If *I* can stay captivated for a full day in this process, you probably can too.

I think my personal journey will help illustrate what this time of preparation can be like. When we ran the carpet cleaning business in Fort Worth, I knew God had called me, but I only had a foggy idea of what His plan was. But He gave me certain steps to follow, and I learned I couldn't move forward if I failed to follow one of His steps.

First, He told me to sell the business. That was frightening to even think about, but I did it.

Next, we moved back to Florida, near Missy's family, and I started the drywall construction business. As the business was growing, I knew He had more for me. "Lord," I prayed, "what do You want me to learn in this season of preparation?"

All He told me was, "Learn My Word."

So I listened to the Bible on audiocassette. As I mentioned previously, when I was working seventy hours per week, I heard the whole Bible in just one week. My favorite version was what I called the Darth Vader edition, read by James Earl Jones.

I found this desire to learn more, to go deeper into understanding it. I listened to the expositional version, which went verse by verse, explaining each one. I did this for five years. I loved it! I knew I was being prepared for something, but I didn't know what. I only knew I did not want to miss the opportunity when it came by being unprepared in His Word.

While He was preparing me spiritually, He was also working on us financially, guiding us in the handling of our money with the clear message: get out of debt.

God opened the door to full-time ministry as soon as we eliminated all debt.

Part of the preparation was learning how to operate in a ministry and church setting. I did a bunch of volunteer work and honed in on what God had gifted me to do—help people with their finances.

> God opened the door to full-time ministry as soon as we eliminated all debt.

He sent me to Richland Hills Church of Christ where I served as stewardship pastor for two years. It was a phenomenal experience. I was trained as the pastoral staff poured their love, experience and knowledge into me. I got to watch how healthy leadership functions and works together over long periods of time. While I was serving, I was also learning and being trained up for the next part of His plan.

He opened the door to Gateway where all that background and preparation is needed on a daily basis, and where I have the privilege and opportunity to work with fantastic ministers in an amazing move of God. I am soaking up all I possibly can from them.

I don't know what my future holds, but my heart's desire is to be a life-long servant at Gateway Church. Here, I believe I am using all my gifts and fulfilling my calling.

Life Seasons

The final piece of Life Stewardship is Life Seasons. As we progress through life, we go through various times or seasons.

There is a concept out in the world called retirement. I think this is a disservice to people, even a lie. There is no model in Scripture for an unproductive life filled with relaxation. I believe God envisions us being always useful and doing things for Him right up until Jesus comes.

But the world's attitude seems to be: "I'll suffer through and when I retire, then I'll do what I really want to do—what I really like to do."

That's baloney.

I am all for retirement, but not as an end. It is a season where we continue to live and serve. We may initiate self-funded mission work. We can use our life-earned wisdom to mentor the next generation. Retirement is a time to live a life of significance. Many people living for retirement goals never find their *today* goals. They miss years of today goals focusing only on living in retirement years.

Here is my favorite retirement verse:

Psalm 92:14 (NLT)
Even in old age they will still produce fruit; they will remain vital and green.

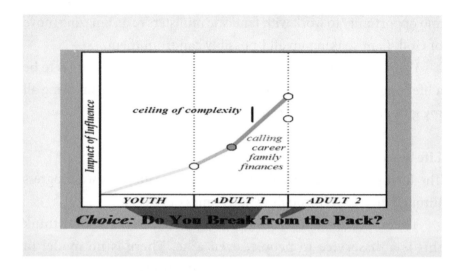

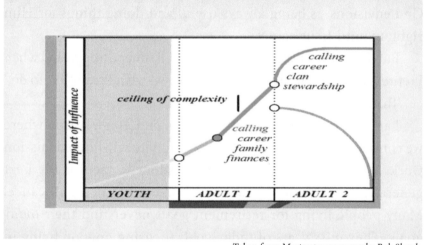

Taken from Mastersprogram.org by Bob Shank.

Life could be divided into three seasons.

1. Youth

    a. Childhood – Education

2. Early Adult

    a. Marriage – Empty Nest

    b. Career

c. Search for Calling

d. Somewhere in this season – "Halftime"

3. Golden Adult

a. Empty Nest to Glory

b. "Retirement Years"

There are three seasons of life. The first eighteen to twenty-two years is our youth. This is when we do the bulk of our learning. We're in school, and we don't have a lot of control.

Let's call the second season Adult One. This is the first phase of adulthood. This usually lasts from when we get married until we become "empty nesters." We meet our spouse, launch our careers and raise our families. This is also a time when we search for our calling. But the search can become muted as we get caught up in managing the day-to-day aspects of life. We find a place to serve that fits our lifestyle, but it may not be what God has called us to do.

Adult Two is when we reach the "empty nest." This is where some people experience their "Mid-Life Crisis." They're frustrated because life hasn't been what they expected it would be. I think it's because they're doing something they're giftings don't line up with, so they're dissatisfied. This is where a life of doing nothing after retirement looks very tempting. Just play golf and chill out.

Let me encourage you. Adult Two is when you can pour yourself into your calling instead of retiring. You can aim at what God's called you to do, and you can make an eternal difference.

Many people, when they reach sixty, are in their peak leadership time. With their experience and knowledge, they are hitting on all cylinders.

Our culture sees retirement as a time to slack off, and I think that's a disservice to the Body of Christ. Retirement is when you are most useful, when people look up to you for who you are and what you bring to the Body.

I think people should have their mid-life crisis when they're in their teens because then they would be free to focus on what God has called them to do. They can live a life that never aims for retirement because they don't want to retire. They may leave their "job" or their "career," but they'll never stop working.

We all go through seasons in life. Solomon said it this way in Ecclesiastes 3:1–14.

There is a time for everything,
and a season for every activity under the heavens:
   a time to be born and a time to die,
   a time to plant and a time to uproot,
   a time to kill and a time to heal,
   a time to tear down and a time to build,
   a time to weep and a time to laugh,
   a time to mourn and a time to dance,
   a time to scatter stones and a time to gather them,
   a time to embrace and a time to refrain from embracing,
   a time to search and a time to give up,
   a time to keep and a time to throw away,
   a time to tear and a time to mend,
   a time to be silent and a time to speak,
   a time to love and a time to hate,
   a time for war and a time for peace.

What do workers gain from their toil? I have seen the burden God has laid on the human race. He has made everything beautiful in its time. He has also set eternity in the human heart; yet no one can fathom what God has done from beginning to end. I know there is nothing better for people than to be happy and do good while they live. That each of them may eat and drink and find satisfaction in all their toil—this is the gift of God. I know everything God does will endure forever; nothing can be added to it and nothing taken from it.

I think the idea of setting eternity in our hearts is why death seems so unnatural to us. We're not wired for death. We're wired for life. God created us to live forever.

Sin created a short lifespan. Every time someone dies, no matter what their age, it always feels like a period in the middle of a sentence.

If I'm successful in teaching these concepts, you're going to aggressively pursue financial freedom so you can do whatever God has put on your heart.

Here's another formula:

- Begin with your **identity**—who you are in Christ.
- Add your **gifting**—which you discover by becoming a student of *you*.
- Join them with **timing**—watch for God.
- Add **preparation**—figure out how to discern God's voice and begin moving in the direction He calls you to.
- Bring your **life season** into it—know what season you're in and plan accordingly.

This will lead to a powerful life of stewardship.

PRACTICAL APPLICATIONS

There's one area we've touched on in each chapter, sometimes hard, sometimes not so hard as the lesson required. That area is communication. As we near the end, I want to share an eight-point communication process. It's a process that can be used in any area, but is especially useful in handling money.

One of the keys to a successful life of stewardship is discussing and planning your finances with your spouse.

As I mentioned earlier, money was the worst area of communication for Missy and I. Now it's our best. This process evolved over seventeen years of marriage. It works.

First, it's a **team effort**. When the paycheck comes in, we sit down and do the Spending Plan. We give each dollar a place. Every dollar has a job to do. It strengthens the marriage if both spouses know where the money is going.

One spouse handling the money only creates tension and resentment. When husband and wife create a team, both know where the money is going and this builds not only a firm financial foundation, it builds trust and unity in the marriage.

Second, **know the condition of your flocks**. This applies to more than just the budget. Know where everything is in your finances. Being a bit geeky, I prepared a PowerPoint presentation that showed Missy where everything is. If something should happen to me while I'm traveling, she'll have all the information she needs to handle our financial situation.

Third, the **thirty-dollar rule**. We have an agreement not to spend more than $30 on an item if we have not discussed it previously. If we find something we want to purchase, we call or text each other. It's not about asking permission; it's for accountability to each other and to the spending plan we're both committed to. I may find something I'd like to get. When I check in with Missy, she reminds me of something I've forgotten about. This rule helps us to stay disciplined and on track.

Fourth, periodically take a **vision retreat**. We take some time away to talk about where we're going with our finances and in life. This is "us" time away from the kids and work. This is time where we press into the Lord together, sharing what He is speaking to each of us.

I mentioned at the beginning of this book that Missy asked me if money were no object, what I would do with my life. I responded that I would teach what the Bible says about money. This happened on one of our vision retreats. I don't know if she would have asked it otherwise, but it allowed me to share my heart. When the job offer came, the description matched exactly what we had outlined on that retreat. The retreat helped us to recognize the Lord's confirmation when it came.

At least once a year, set aside time to discuss your goals and why you're doing the things you do. These things will help you to stay in touch with each other.

It doesn't have to be expensive, although it makes for a special treat if you can afford something nice.

Fifth, **set long-terms goals**. Keep your long-term goals in the forefront so they can determine today's spending decisions. As you know, our goal is to live on 1/3 of our income, give 1/3 and save 1/3. To get to that point is going to take determination, discipline and careful planning.

Our long-term goals guide us in setting short-term goals.

If you have kids, involve them in your goal setting. It will help them understand the basic principles of financial management and the decisions you and your spouse make. It helps them be a part of the process and take some ownership and responsibility for achieving the goals. It's awesome for them to see the outcomes you've discussed as a family.

> Our long-term goals guide us in setting short-term goals.

This is another area where working together makes the marriage stronger as the two of you work on your goals.

Sixth—this one is for the married guys—**spoil your wife**. It's not just buying stuff for her, although that is part of it. It's an attitude we develop about her. The Bible refers to it as honoring your wife. It's the little things like holding doors. It's asking yourself, *"How do I treat her?"*

Once, Missy was on a mission trip to India, and I decided to surprise her. We had planned on installing wood floors. We budgeted and purchased the materials. We just hadn't decided on when. While she was away, I called the contractor and had it done. The challenge was hiding the ongoing mess in the house during her Skype calls to me and the kids, but we pulled it off.

When I spoil my wife, she feels honored, and I set an example for my children.

Seventh—this one is for the married ladies—**adapt to your husband**. I enjoy bike riding—long-distance bike riding. Missy began bike riding with me. She'll tell you she's a girly-girl. Riding in Texas heat and sweating is just not her thing. But she does it, and it is a precious time for us to hang out and have fun together. She's even gone on some long-distance bike races with me and done pretty well.

It also helped our marriage and finances. It gave her more insight into how I'm wired. She could understand some of the things I might need.

And, adapting to your spouse becomes something you can do together which strengthens your relationship. And being together improves communication.

The eighth step is for the married men as well. **Be gentle and create security**. The man sets the tone in the household. If I'm rattled or panicked about finances, or anything else for that matter, it can make Missy and the kids feel insecure. If Dad's losing it, there must be big trouble.

If the man stays calm, the family stays calm.

Let me share a story about how staying calm helped a shepherd control his sheep. NATO tank exercises were held in the area of Germany where this man lived. People noticed that when the cannon was fired, the sheep would look at the shepherd. He stayed calm and so did the sheep. They took their cue from him.

The family is the same way. They will take their cue from the head.

God created men to handle a lot of stress and pressure. We naturally handle it fairly well—most of the time.

Creating this sense of security works in business and ministry as well.

What's the secret to handling stress and pressure? When they come at me, I turn around and hand it to the Lord. He is the one who creates the security. I just walk in it.

CHAPTER NINE

LAW OF ETERNAL REWARDS

MANAGING OUR ETERNAL INVESTMENTS

Martin Luther once wrote, "There are two days on my calendar—Today and That Day."

The commentator Matthew Henry wrote, "It ought to be the business of every day to prepare for our last day."

Our eternal reward is the why behind all stewardship.

We can be really good with our money, keep our budget balanced, pay off our debt and save a bunch. We can be living in the fullness of our calling. But, if we've never really understood the law of rewards in Scripture, we've missed out on opportunities to invest in eternity.

Everything we do in life leads up to one moment in our future. Everything we believe, everything we do, every decision we make—including financial—leads up to our final review.

In school, I dreaded reviews and tests. I didn't do well in a lot of subjects because I didn't pay attention and was easily distracted. I would come to class unprepared and pay the consequences, like a 33 semester average in geometry. If the subject interested me, I would do quite well. I aced government, history and economics.

When I knew what was expected of me and liked the topic, I had a totally different attitude. I was ready and eager. "Bring it on."

God has the ultimate timeline. Imagine your whole life, from birth to death, laid out, each event marked and open to view. It will show the great things we accomplished and the seasons we went through. It will also show the opportunities we had and missed. Nothing catches Him by surprise.

The comfort is our sins won't be there because He doesn't remember them.

Hebrews 12:1–2 describes the great crowd of witnesses in heaven watching us and cheering us on. Things that happen on earth are on full display in heaven.

James 4:14 tells us our life is like a vapor, a morning fog. It's here a little while, then, it's gone. But in heaven, it means something forever, and it's recorded.

In this chapter, I want to prepare you for your final review that will take place in heaven. We're going to examine several of what I call Final Review Prep Questions. I'll list them here, and we'll go deeper into each one in the following pages.

1. Will Jesus hold us accountable for the way we steward our lives? Briefly, yes, He will.
2. Do our works result in salvation? No, the Bible doesn't teach our works can earn our way into heaven.
3. Can we earn and lose our rewards? Yes and yes.
4. What is "Treasure in Heaven?" (We'll explore how we can build up our treasure in heaven.)
5. Can I change my eternal portfolio? Can I make a

difference? Can I actually do something today that changes my whole eternity? Yes, yes and yes.

6. What happens after I die? Keep reading; I will show you.
7. Is heaven more than endless singing and fat babies on puffy clouds? It sure is.

As I mentioned before, when I was young, my parents were very involved in a small church. My Mom was on the praise and worship team. They sang *a cappella* style.

One day, driving home from church, I asked her, "Mom, what's heaven gonna be like?"

She said, "It's going to be glorious, just endless praise and singing."

I didn't say anything to that, and after a while, my Mom asked, "Why the silence?"

"Well, crud," I said. "I don't like our singing. Are we gonna be able to do anything else in heaven?"

The idea of eternal singing of all "twenty-five stanzas" of Amazing Grace *a cappella* is not my idea of fun.

My wife would love singing the whole time. She has a beautiful gifting in this area. I'm not wired that way.

TWO JUDGMENT SEATS

There are two different judgments for different groups. We born-again Christians will face what is called, in Greek, the Bema Seat of Judgment.

In 2 Corinthians 5:10 (NASB) we read, *"For we must all appear before the **judgment seat of Christ**, so that each one may be recompensed for his deeds in the body, according to what he has done, whether good or bad."(emphasis added)*

Romans 14:10–12 (NASB) reinforces this: *"For we will all stand before the judgment seat of God. For it is written, 'As I live, says the Lord, every knee shall bow to me, and every tongue shall give praise to God.' So then each one of us will give an account of himself to God."*

Think of the Bema Seat as a raised dais with steps leading up to it. When Pilate judged Jesus, He was sitting on a bema seat.

In Scripture, the Bema Seat is where Jesus will reward us and where we might possibly lose our rewards. Revelation 22:12 (NLT) tells us, *"Look, I am coming soon, bringing my reward with me to repay all people according to their deeds."*

This seat is different than the judgment most people think about.

When most of us hear judgment, we think of **The Great White Throne Judgment** as described in Revelation 20:11–15 (NASB):

> *Then I saw a great white throne and Him who sat upon it, from whose presence earth and heaven fled away, and no place was found for them. And I saw the dead, the great and the small, standing before the throne, and books were opened; and another book was opened, which is the book of life; and the dead were judged from the things which were written in the books, according to their deeds. And the sea gave up the dead which were in it, and death and Hades gave up the dead which were in them; and they were judged, every one of them according to their deeds. Then death and Hades were thrown into the lake of fire. This is the second death, the lake of fire. And if anyone's name was not found written in the book of life, he was thrown into the lake of fire.*

The Bema Seat is for believers.

The Great White Throne is not part of our future. We will see it, but those of us in Christ are immediately with Him.

I mentioned earlier that God has the ultimate timeline for us. He knows the destination of the saints because He can see from the beginning to end all at the same time. We can't. God is like a person watching a parade from a rooftop or helicopter. He can see the whole thing. You and I are like a person standing on a sidewalk, watching the same parade. From our vantage point, we can only see a few feet in either direction. Because we live in this time domain, our view is skewed. We can't see all that God sees.

How do we make sure our names are in the Lamb's book of life? It's as simple as John 3:16—reading it and believing it and welcoming God into our life through the sacrifice that Jesus paid for our sins.

> God knows the destination of the saints because He can see from the beginning to end all at the same time.

It's that simple. And it's also complicated because there are two types of faith, and sometimes we get them confused. I'll explain them to you.

TWO TYPES OF FAITH

Ascentia is one kind. It is the mental acknowledgment of something's existence. The demons acknowledge and believe God exists.

Fiducia is more than mental acknowledgment. It involves a trust in something; a giving over to it; a complete believing and acceptance of something. This is the kind of faith a Christian has in Christ.

We exercise fiducia when we sit in a chair. We don't stand and ponder the chair for ten minutes. We don't pick it up and examine its structure. We don't push on the legs to make sure they're secure. We don't look for missing screws. No, we just sit down on the thing expecting it to hold us without even thinking about it.

A Christian has fiducia when he has real faith and trust in Christ, not simply an acknowledgment that He lived on earth at one time.

Another way to put it is, there are many people in the world who believe Jesus existed. This is ascentia. But they do not believe He is their Savior—the one to be looked to and trusted for the forgiveness of their sin.

Ascentia does not lead to works. Fiducia does.

Ascentia is not of the heart. Fiducia is.

Let me be very clear here. We are not saved by our good works. We are saved *TO DO* good works.

The work of Jesus saved us. Our works, once we're saved, reward us.

TREASURES IN HEAVEN

Matthew 6:19–24

"Do not store up for yourselves treasures on earth, where moth and rust destroy, and where thieves break in and steal. But store up for yourselves treasures in heaven, where moth does not destroy and where thieves do not break in and steal. For where your treasure is, there your heart will be also. The eye is the lamp of the body. If your eyes are good, your whole body will be full of light. But if your eyes are bad, your whole body will be full of darkness. If then the light within you is darkness, how great is that darkness! No one can serve two masters. Either he will hate the one and love the other, or he will be devoted to the one and despise the other. You cannot serve both God and Money."

How do we do it? How do we build up our treasure in heaven?

Paul tells us in 1 Timothy 6:18–19:

Command them to do good, to be rich in good deeds, and to be generous and willing to share. In this way they will lay up treasure for themselves as a firm foundation for the coming age, so that they may take hold of the life that is truly life.

Being rich in good deeds, being willing to share and help others as God directs, is one of the ways we convert or transfer our treasure into eternity.

In Matthew 19:21, Jesus answered the rich, young ruler: *"If you want to be perfect, go, sell your possessions and give to the poor, and you will have treasure in heaven. Then come, follow me."*

Jesus was talking about eternal investing. What we do here gives us opportunities in heaven.

Let's look at some of the ways God rewards us.

He will reward generously.

Matthew 19:29 (NASB)
"And everyone who has left houses or brothers or sisters or father or mother or children or farms for My name's sake, will receive as many times as much, and will inherit eternal life."

When we give up things for His sake, to be obedient to His call, He will reward us both here and in heaven. God rewards us for what we do, not what we believe.

Matthew 16:27 (NASB)
"For the Son of Man is going to come in the glory of His Father with His angels, and will then repay every man according to his deeds."

God rewards us for kindness to the undeserving, for those who are mean to us, even those who reject our gifts.

Luke 6:35 (NASB)
"But love your enemies, and do good, and lend, expecting nothing in return; and your reward will be great, and you will be sons of the Most High; for He Himself is kind to ungrateful and evil men."

Having a gift rejected is one of the most harmful and hurtful things we can experience. And God knows all about gifts not being received and being spit upon. He's experienced that. He gave His only Son just to have Him rejected and crucified.

He rewards us when we care for those in need, especially physical needs.

Mark 9:41 (NASB)
"For whoever gives you a cup of water to drink because of your name as followers of Christ, truly I say to you, he will not lose his reward."

When I get my wife a drink at the dinner table, I'm meeting her need and God recognizes this.

God rewards us when we care for those too poor or incapacitated to pay us back.

Luke 14:12–14 (NASB)
And He also went on to say to the one who had invited Him, "When you give a luncheon or dinner, do not invite your friends or your brothers or your relatives or rich neighbors, otherwise they may also invite you in return and that will be your repayment. But when you give a reception, invite the poor, the crippled, the lame, the blind, and you will be blessed since they do not have the means to repay you; for you will be repaid at the resurrection of the righteous."

This verse takes on a whole new meaning for me when I think of my family's trip to India and the poverty and devastation in Mumbai.

God rewards us when we are wise and productive in using the resources and opportunities He gives us. I don't know about you, but when I get to heaven, I long to hear God say, *"Well done, my good and faithful servant."* (Matthew 25:20–21)

He rewards us for being persecuted for Christ.

Luke 6:22–24

"Blessed are you when people hate you, when they exclude you and insult you and reject your name as evil, because of the Son of Man. Rejoice in that day and leap for joy, because great is your reward in heaven. For that is how their ancestors treated the prophets. But woe to you who are rich, for you have already received your comfort."

Have you ever had someone really go after you because of your belief in Christ? Attacking your beliefs; calling you a liar? It's pretty frustrating because they're hard to reason with. When it happened to me, it made me angry because not only were they lying about me, they were attacking my God. I know I'm supposed to turn the other cheek. It's not always easy, but when I do, the result will be a reward in heaven.

God also rewards us for identifying with those suffering for Christ and for taking material loss.

Hebrews 10:34–35

You suffered along with those in prison and joyfully accepted the confiscation of your property, because you knew that you yourselves had better and lasting possessions. So do not throw away your confidence; it will be richly rewarded.

You need to persevere so that when you have done the will of God, you will receive what He has promised.

All over the world, our brothers and sisters in the Lord are being persecuted for their faith and martyred every day. In comparison, we have it easy here. The suffering of fellow believers for their faith adds reality to my prayers for them.

ETERNAL CROWNS

1 Corinthians 9:24–25
Do you not know that in a race all runners run, but only one gets the prize? Run in such a way as to win the prize. Everyone who competes in the games goes into strict training. They do it to get a crown that will not last; but we do it to get a crown that will last forever.

What are these crowns awaiting us in heaven? I've been able to identify five eternal crowns.

The Crown of Righteousness
This is for those who believe in His appearing.

2 Timothy 4:8 (NLT)
And now the prize awaits me—the crown of righteousness, which the Lord, the righteous Judge, will give me on the day of his return. And the prize is not just for me but for all who look forward to his appearing.

The Crown of Glory
This crown is for those who feed the flock and who volunteer in the church, serving and meeting the needs of the faithful.

1 Peter 5:2–4 (NLT)
Care for the flock that God has entrusted to you. Watch over it willingly, not grudgingly—not for what you will get

out of it but because you are eager to serve God. Don't lord it over the people assigned to your care, but lead them by your good example. And when the Good Shepherd appears, you will receive a crown of never-ending glory and honor.

The Crown of Life

This is reserved for those who have suffered for His sake.

Revelation 2:10 (NLT)

Don't be afraid of what you are about to suffer. The devil will throw some of you into prison to test you ... If you remain faithful even when facing death, I will give you the crown of life.

The Crown of Rejoicing

Soul winners and evangelists will receive this crown.

1 Thessalonians 2:19–20 (NKJV)

For what is our hope, or joy, or crown of rejoicing? Is it not even you in the presence of our Lord Jesus Christ at His coming? For you are our glory and joy.

The Incorruptible Crown

This crown will be given to those who pressed on steadfast through persecutions and trials.

1 Corinthians 9:25–27

Everyone who competes in the games goes into strict training. They do it to get a crown that will not last, but we do it to get a crown that will last forever. Therefore I do not run like someone running aimlessly; I do not fight like a boxer beating the air. No, I strike a blow to my body and make it my slave so that after I have preached to others, I myself will not be disqualified for the prize.

A crown that will last forever? I wonder what it will look like. Actually, it's beyond our wildest imagination.

NEGATIVE ASPECTS OF THE JUDGMENT OF WORKS

We're not talking salvation here. We're talking post-salvation and our works, both good and bad.

Some Christians will not hear, "Well done, good and faithful servant" (Matthew 25:21). There are going to be differing rewards when we get to heaven. We're not all going to be equal. We'll all be in heaven, but we'll have different things.

Some Christians will be ashamed when they meet Jesus. Surprised?

1 John 2:28
And now, dear children, continue in him so that when he appears we may be confident and unashamed before him at his coming.

Our salvation is secure even if we live in sin. The Holy Spirit can convict us to move out of that sin, but what if we die before we can achieve it. We are never cast away. The Prodigal Son wasn't. He just didn't have any rewards.

In heaven, some Christians will "suffer loss."

1 Corinthians 3:12–15
If anyone builds on this foundation using gold, silver, costly stones, wood, hay or straw, their work will be shown for what it is, because the Day will bring it to light. It will be

revealed with fire, and the fire will test the quality of each person's work. If what has been built survives, the builder will receive a reward. If it is burned up, the builder will suffer loss but yet will be saved—even though only as one escaping through the flames.

Fire will test the quality of each person's work. If what we built survives, we will receive a reward. If it burns up, the builder will suffer loss but will be saved from the flames. The builder is still saved, but because he never quite made time for the Lord, he suffers loss of rewards.

At the Bema Judgment Seat of Christ, Christians will experience the consequences of the good they failed to do and the bad they did do.

2 Corinthians 5:10 (NLT)
For we must all stand before Christ to be judged. We will each receive whatever we deserve for the good or evil we have done in this earthly body.

Colossians 3:25 (NLT)
But if you do what is wrong, you will be paid back for the wrong you have done. For God has no favorites.

Jesus will wipe away all the tears in heaven—tears of missed opportunity in this life.

We will not be judged for sin in the work of eternal salvation. All sin—confessed and unconfessed—has been taken care of by the work of the Cross. We will never stand against that sin at Judgment.

Hebrews 10:14 (NLT)
For by that one offering he forever made perfect those who are being made holy.

Justification is a one-time thing, settled forever at the Cross.

Sanctification, on the other hand, is a moving target. We're continuing to grow and progress in our walk with Christ. It will never end until the day we die. We will never reach the point—in this life—where we can say, "I am completely sanctified." An attitude like that probably requires a humility test. We experience full sanctification when we die and go to heaven.

> Justification is a one-time thing, settled forever at the Cross.

Through Jesus, many are made righteous (Romans 5:19).

He forgives our sins and remembers them no more (Hebrews 8:12).

He does not remember our "sins and lawless deeds" (Hebrews 10:17–18).

There is no longer any offering for sin. This doesn't give us the liberty to live as heathens. We will lose our rewards if we do (1 Corinthians 3:12–15).

We live as free men and women, focused on the eternal gain that awaits us (2 Corinthians 4:16–18).

WHAT'S HEAVEN REALLY LIKE?

Have you ever daydreamed about what heaven is like? Wish you could have a peek? We can tell a few things about it by looking at Scripture.

Heaven is an actual physical place. Christ has traveled to and from it. So have angels, and in rare circumstances, people, prior to their deaths, have traveled there (John 1:32, 6:33; Acts 1:2; Matthew 28:2; Revelation 10:1; 2 Kings 2:11; 2 Corinthians 12:2; Revelation 11:12, 21:1–2).

Heaven has light, water, trees, fruit and animals (Isaiah 11:6–7; Revelation 6:2; 7:9, 17; 19:11; 21:23–25; 22:1–2, 14).

Even heaven is going to get a remodel. Revelation tells us there will be a new heaven and a new earth. We should be able to move back and forth between them and bring things with us. The new earth will be different too. We can have fast bikes and cars with no worries about accidents or tickets (or running out of gas).

Heaven is a city (Hebrews 11:16, 12:22, 13:14; Revelation 21:2).

In heaven, the city's gates are always open, and people will travel in and out, some bringing treasures into the city (Revelation 21:24–25, 22:14).

In heaven, we will worship God and serve Him and rule with Him (Revelation 5:11–13, 7:15, 22:5). We'll have face-to-face communication with Him.

We'll also have rest from our earthly labors (Revelation 14:13). We'll be doing things in heaven, but those activities won't exhaust us.

There will be times of celebration and fellowship, time to eat and drink. Our resurrected bodies will be able to eat and drink. Jesus ate with the apostles on the beach after He rose from the dead. Abraham cooked and served a meal for angels who visited him, and they ate.

Jesus described heaven as having many rooms or dwellings. Places He—the Creator—will prepare for us Himself (John 14:2–3). He knows everything we like. Our homes will be perfect for us. All we see on this earth will be in the new earth only in much, much better fashion.

Our imagination is the only thing that limits us in dreaming what heaven will be like.

We can have small groups and throw parties. We'll have a whole eternity of finding new things.

I imagine our entry into heaven to be like the last scene in the first Star Wars movie where Luke, Leia and Han climb the podium to find a sea of people cheering and celebrating their arrival. We'll see family and friends who have gone before us. We'll meet the people we've read about in Scripture. This makes me cautious when I speak negatively about Biblical characters. I may have to stand in front of someone like David and explain what I meant.

Heaven is the place and time when all righteous acts—many of which were disregarded and even punished on earth—will finally be rewarded.

The prospect of what is waiting for us in heaven is what motivates us to move forward, to get all our finances in order. It motivates us to make wise decisions, to find our calling, to get in the financial position to pursue what God is doing in our lives. It drives us to be like the servant who was given five talents and earned five more. We don't want to be the servant who took his one talent and buried it.

We want to fulfill all that God has called us to be and do. Christian writer McNair Wilson once said, "If you don't do you, God's creation goes unfinished."

God didn't call me to be Billy Graham or Pastor Robert Morris of Gateway Church. When I stand in front of the Bema Seat of Christ, He's going to ask, "Were you the Gunnar I called you to be?"

> If you don't do you, God's creation goes unfinished.

I want to be able to say with all my heart, "Yes."

And then hear Him say, "Well done, good and faithful servant." And with a sweep of His arm, He'll say, "Enter and receive your reward."

What is the Lord speaking to you about all this?

CHAPTER TEN

FOR PASTORS AND CHURCH LEADERS

Where do you go from here? My goal is for pastors and church leaders to apply the principles in this book in their own churches—but not just as a new program or curriculum tacked on to existing education efforts. You may not be a pastor or church leader yet, but please consider God may use you to spark a financial freedom revival in your church.

Picture in your mind what your church would look like if your people were financially free. Dwell on that image. Dwell on the impact your financially-free congregation could have on your community, on the world.

Stewardship ministry is an integral part of making that happen.

The hope of the world isn't politics or economics. If the government could really fix the economy, every president would have a good economy. Our country is in trouble, and the only solution is transformed lives through Jesus Christ.

The hope of the world is Jesus Christ. The Church, as the Bride of Christ, is the force to bring this hope to the world.

The Church plays three vital roles in making this happen.

First, we are like the *Mayo Clinic*. People show up hurting and don't know why. We diagnose, help them get healed and build a solid foundation.

Second, we're like the *Pentagon*. We've been given a worldwide strategy and mission. We hear from our Commander-in-Chief in heaven, and we do what He tells us.

Finally, we're like *a military base*. We bring in the recruits—the believers, and we train and equip them. Then we send them out to shine the light of their freedom, including their financial freedom.

Our society is in a moral free-fall, but the Word of God is SOLID and living. We have to band together as financial professionals to work with God to reverse this course.

HEALING THE WOUNDED

Early in this book, I discussed church members who have been hurt by improper teaching of stewardship and generosity. But this hurt has also been inflicted on pastors and church leaders by other pastors and ministers who abused you and misused your gifts and your giving and left you hurt. There are many walking wounded among us because of what the Church has done.

> Our society is in a moral free-fall, but the Word of God is SOLID and living.

As a stewardship pastor and a representative of the stewardship ministry, I want to apologize. You've been wounded because well-meaning pastors were not trained properly. And, because of the role you play in your churches, the damage can be even greater than among the congregation.

Allow me to pray for you.

Father, I know You've purposed each and every one of us to do something great in Your Kingdom. Lord, I ask You to bring to mind past wounds and hurts we've experienced in the church world around finances. I pray You give us the strength to forgive and set things aside, even if we think we've already done that. Holy Spirit, bring to light the things that arise in our hearts that cause us to flinch when the church talks about money.

Lord, I pray for my brothers and sisters in the pastorate that they would have a revelation of what Your Word says about money.

And, Lord, I pray Your healing word will rest on those who read these words, and that we will completely clear the deck and start over, walking in unity, powerfully advancing Your Kingdom. Amen.

THE PASTOR'S PERSPECTIVE

Let's take a look at how pastors perceive ministry.

52% of pastors say they and their spouses believe that being in pastoral ministry is hazardous to their family's well-being and health.

56% of pastors' wives say they have no close friends.

57% would leave the pastorate if they had somewhere else to go or some other vocation they could do.

70% don't have any close friends.

90% feel unqualified or poorly prepared for ministry. (I think we're always going to feel that way.) The Holy Spirit is never going to let us get ahead of Him to the point where we say, "I've got it, Lord." He won't let us step out in our own pride to do God's work.

94% of pastors feel pressure to have a perfect family.

1,500 pastors leave their ministries every month due to burnout, conflict or moral failure.

I believe that pastors can help and support each other and that you, as pastors, associate pastors and church leaders can work together to change these numbers and guide your church into new areas of spiritual, physical and financial growth.

When the culture of stewardship and the spirit of generosity rise up in the church, things change. The church becomes stronger. The Enemy will attack to stop the church and the financial world from working together in ministry. He will try to sow strife and division. God wants us as ministers and church leaders to work with our pastors to defeat these attacks and to advance our ministries.

WHY A MINISTRY OF STEWARDSHIP AND GENEROSITY?

First, because it is God's heart for people. It's not something God wants *from* you. It's something God wants *for* you, for His people.

This is why we teach this material; why we work to give people a solid foundation of who they are in Christ in the area of finances.

> When the culture of stewardship and the spirit of generosity rise up in the church, things change.

To do this successfully, our motives must be pure.

It is the pursuit of the spirit of mammon to say, "If our church had more money, we would be successful." Congregations who do this chase unrighteous mammon and serve a counterfeit god.

God has never told anyone, "You need more money," *or* "Your church needs more money. And when you have it, then you can do all I've called you to do." He has never made money a condition of success or a sign of holiness. Money is one of the tools He provides to carry out His work, but His work can be achieved without money by those whose hearts are open to serving Him.

Why teach stewardship and generosity? It's Biblical. If, as a pastor, I'm charged to teach the full wisdom of God, I'm definitely going into the scriptures on money to ensure I'm getting it right. There are 2,300 scriptures on money. Seventeen of the thirty-eight parables Jesus taught are on money and possessions.

A lot of Christians are shocked to learn there is so much about money in the Bible. It's shocking to many non-Christians as well.

On a trip recently, I was seated next to a well-dressed, obviously successful man who wore Buddhist jewelry. I asked what he did for a living, and he told me he oversaw a large region for a car manufacturer.

> His work can be achieved without money by those whose hearts are open to serving Him.

Then he asked me what I did for a living. (I was so glad he asked.)

I smiled and told him, "I'm an eternal investment broker." Then I explained that I'm a pastor who teaches what the Bible says about money.

I could tell by his expression he was thinking, *"How can I get out of this conversation?"* Fortunately, he was blocked in the middle seat.

As I talked about the scriptures and parables, he became fascinated. I quoted scriptures and shared principles I knew he would recognize from his business acumen. I shared the roles of God and Christ in our lives and finances.

I could tell he was interested. I didn't realize how interested until he tracked me down at the car rental center. He wanted to exchange cards, and we made plans to stay in touch.

When we teach on money, we need to first go through the exercise with our leadership team. They need to be prepared and understand God's plan in this area.

When I first started teaching churches how to build a stewardship ministry, they didn't have a heart for stewardship ministry. It wasn't a big deal to them in the early part of this century. It was added to the cart of other things the church offered. It frequently got lost in all the other stuff churches did, especially if people had been wounded and resented teaching on money.

Then the economy shifted. Pastors came to me, needing help. "Our budget's a mess." "We have to lay off staff." "Stewardship is going to raise money for us, right?" It wasn't that their questions were bad, but they had the wrong motivation.

Now that everyone has pretty much adapted to the new normal, even though the economy is still not great, the questions and attitude are different. The atmosphere in churches is changing. The realization is dawning that stewardship and generosity could really change lives. Now pastors ask, "How do we establish a stewardship ministry in our church? I think it will change lives." This excited me!

Now is the time to sit down with your pastor and ministry team and ask, "What do we want for the people of our church?"

There are seven things we want to see in the people of Gateway Church at all levels of the stewardship ministry.

> The realization is dawning that stewardship and generosity could really change lives.

We want them to have **Christ-centered financial views**. We want them to wear the Biblical principles of stewardship like a contact lens so they see everything through it.

We want them to be **generous in their tithes and offerings**. We unapologetically teach on giving because we know what it's going to do in their lives. Money given to Gateway will result in souls in the Kingdom.

We want our people to **experience margin**, to live in such a way they have money left over at the end of each pay period.

We want everyone to be **debt-free**. We teach and counsel them in how to develop a plan to get there. Being out of debt creates margin and gives emotional and psychological as well as financial freedom.

We want them to be **savers**. The Bible says we're fools if we don't save. We don't want a bunch of fools around our church. We teach the principles of saving for the short-, medium- and long-term. We want them to save because we have fun when we're saving and seeing the margin increase. We save in order to be givers in every area of life.

We want them to live on a **spending plan**, assigning every dollar a task.

Finally, we want them to be **life stewards**, operating in their strengths and giftings. Once, I met with an accountant who didn't like what he did. He wasn't detailed-oriented. The job was not a fit for him, although he had created a successful practice over the years! Running numbers had simply never been his passion. He went into accounting because it was a family tradition. He followed his father and brother into the profession. He wasn't wired by God to be an accountant.

I'm a strong advocate of personality assessments. There are three I recommend: StrengthsFinder, DiSC Profile and TTI Success Indicators. My accountant friend took these assessments and learned he was *not* wired to crunch numbers all day long. He shifted his responsibilities in his business and started doing things he was more wired to do, and it removed the burden he was carrying to be the chief number guru. Now he has tailored his role in his business to match his natural strengths.

At Gateway, we believe everyone is a life steward. God has given them talents. My job as the stewardship pastor is to help them identify these gifts and then plant them in the areas they're good at, to get them in the right place.

GOD'S MANAGERS

Another reason to teach this: Stewardship is not something we do, it is who we are. God created us to be stewards.

In Genesis 1:1, we see the principle of God owning everything: *"In the beginning, God created the heaven and the earth."* He's the Creator/Owner.

About twenty-five verses later, we find that He created us to be stewards.

Genesis 1:26
Then God said, "Let us make mankind in our image, in our likeness, so that they may rule over the fish in the sea and the birds in the sky, over the livestock, and all the wild animals, and over all the creatures that move along the ground."

Paul gives a nice summary of why we should teach generosity and stewardship. As I mentioned previously, at the time of this letter, Timothy was a young pastor in Ephesus, a major trade city. He probably had the full range of demographics and socio-economic classes in his congregation. In these verses, Paul gives insight into what to teach the people about money.

1 Timothy 6:17–19
Command those who are rich in this present world not to be arrogant nor to put their hope in wealth, which is so uncertain, but to put their hope in God, who richly provides us with everything for our enjoyment. Command them to do good, to be rich in good deeds, and to be generous and willing to share. In this way they will lay up treasure for themselves as a firm foundation for the coming age, so that they may take hold of the life that is truly life.

166

We want all Gateway people to use this passage as a model for their lives.

WE WILL BE HELD ACCOUNTABLE BY GOD

This is a final reason to teach this. At the end of time, we, as pastors and church leaders, will be held accountable. I don't say this to scare you, but to remind you. When we have a deadline, we tend to work more diligently towards it.

> **2 Corinthians 5:10** (NASB)
> *For we must all appear before the judgment seat of Christ, so that each one may be recompensed for his deeds in the body, according to what he has done, whether good or bad.*

At the end of the day, I am responsible for what I share and teach. I get to train folks at Gateway. I also get to travel around the United States and to foreign countries to train and raise up leaders in this ministry. I am responsible for what they teach.

When you're called to stewardship ministry, you gladly accept it and do the best you can.

In Revelation 2 and 3, Jesus writes letters to seven churches and He uses a phrase that should make all church leaders pay attention. He says, "I know your deeds."

He knows what is going on in each of our churches.

GETTING IT DONE

Let me share with you how we get this done at Gateway Church.

We're not simply building a curriculum, we're building a structure for this ministry that curriculum flows in and out of.

I've been asked: "Are you a Dave Ramsey church, Compass church or a Crown Ministry church?" We are a Jesus church. Crown Ministry,

Compass and Dave Ramsey have great materials that we use and have greatly benefited from them. I love the leaders in all those organizations, but as a pastor, I, and Gateway Church, are called to teach the whole counsel of God, not just specific curriculum.

At Gateway, we divided the congregation into four groups. You may recall them from Chapter 1. We use these terms to make sure we're offering something for everyone.

Building a culture of stewardship and generosity in your church requires you to touch all four of these groups within your own congregation.

The first group is those who are **Struggling**. These families are not making ends meet. At times, we've received eleven hundred phone calls per month from people who are hurting financially.

The second group is made up of those who are **Stable**. They have regular income but many times are one missed paycheck away from disaster.

Group three are those who are **Solid**. They are doing well financially. They're not wealthy, but they are managing their finances and building margin.

The Stable and Solid groups make up 70% of most churches.

The **Surplussed** make up the fourth group. These families and individuals have wealth and a high capacity to build more. They need to be ministered to differently—and not to get anything from them. God gave them gifts of leadership and generosity as well as the gift of building big things for the Kingdom. Sadly, most churches have abused them for their gifts—financial and otherwise.

> Building a culture of stewardship and generosity in your church requires you to touch all groups within your own congregation.

Most churches fall off the rails by overly focusing on the *Struggling*: "They're coming to our church, and we've got to do something with them." Or the church goes to another extreme: "We've got to build some buildings, so let's minister to the *Surplussed*." Yet the majority of church members are in the *Stable* and *Solid* groups.

At Gateway, we've learned to be careful about what we do and how we do it. We make sure we offer ministry to everyone, in ways that best meet their needs for the group they're in.

THE STRUGGLING

The key to ministering to this group is *relationship*. We don't want our stewardship ministry to be seen only as the ministry people go to when they're hurting. When we give benevolence, we try to determine if they are looking to have immediate needs met or if they are looking for a life change. If they want life change, we will use our resources to help them walk through it. If they are one of those families who seem to be in perpetual need, we will work with them to get them on the path to life change.

We have an exciting car donation ministry. We've given away as many as seventy cars in a year. We sell the donated junk cars to pay for repairs on the better cars. This program has cost the church very little dollars. It actually supports itself.

Not all our donation vehicles are cars we give away. In 2008, we received a Lamborghini with 2,800 miles on it. I told the church member we would accept it on two conditions: One, he had to have lunch with me (I wanted to figure out what makes someone who gives away a Lamborghini tick. That is an emotional gift for a man.). The second condition was: we had to test drive the car together.

We've had other exotic cars donated including a Ferrari and a Viper. The staff knows I have a soft spot for these cars, so I frequently get to "play" with them a little, including taking our Senior Pastor, Robert Morris, for a spin. We sell these cars through a high-line auction and designate the money to whatever area the donor desires.

We also help our *Struggling* by providing small groups for accountability and prayer. These close-knit groups really help "life change" work out.

In addition, we have a job board where Gateway members who own businesses post job openings in their companies. And we have career workshops to help people figure out what they're good at.

THE STABLE AND THE SOLID

It's sometimes hard to differentiate the *Stable* from the *Solid*, so much of what we offer is available to both groups. This includes generational classes that meet the specific life season of the group. We use my Route 7 class, Dave Ramsey's Financial Peace University and our versions of the Financial Hope Workshops. My friend, Dave Briggs, at Central Christian East Valley Church in Phoenix, originally created the Financial Hope Workshop. The workshop helps us logistically provide a group counseling service which helps more people at one time than traditional one-on-one counseling. It is a seven-week process where families receive thirty minutes of teaching, then meet in small groups with counselors who walk them through the changes.

We have equipping classes on many different stewardship topics which offer prayer and discipleship with a solid foundation on what the Bible says about money.

Thirty-one different topical classes are taught through our stewardship ministry. We bring in church members who know the topics and we structure the classes to answer three questions:

What do we want them to know?

What Biblical principles do we want them to believe?

What do we want them to do with what they learn in the class?

The classes cover topics ranging from buying a car, to buying a home, to handling your taxes. One class taught couponing. We had standing room only as over one hundred people showed up! After class, the teachers prayed for two hours for those hurting financially. Some of the best ministry we've ever had has been in our couponing classes.

We tie the stewardship ministry in with other Gateway ministries through groups and internal staff training. After we had trained the children's ministry in this area, the youth leaders came back to us with a curriculum they designed to teach stewardship to the youth. It was a fantastic series!

Our marketplace ministry brings in church members who have expertise to teach on different business topics. We are very clear that this is not for them to sell their products or services. It is to share their expertise and to mentor other business leaders and potential leaders. It would be crazy not to use the best business mentors in the church to help others.

THE SURPLUSSED

Those who have wealth are frequently the least pastored group in the church.

At Gateway, we take these men and women on a Journey of Generosity with Generous Living. Check out the website *generousliving.org* for more details. This journey provides deep confirmation of what God is doing in their hearts. Or, it provides a revelation of what God wants to do in their lives.

In our iDisciple program, we give iPods loaded with my favorite sermons from Kingdom Advisors and Generous Living conferences to our high capacity families. We ask that they listen for two weeks, and then I get together with them for lunch. The purpose is not to get money from them. My motive is to minister to them in ways they may not have ever experienced.

> Those who have wealth are frequently the least pastored group in the church.

We plan strategic mission trips with our wealthier families. A few years ago, I took seven men to Israel, asking them to think about ways we could bless the Messianic Body in that country. We had a blast mixing ministry with sightseeing, building relationships with each other and with the leaders of the Messianic Christian community.

These seven men came up with the idea to start a foundation to train entrepreneurs. The foundation would provide nine months of training and mentoring to potential entrepreneurs who applied through their local church and were recommended by their pastor. At the end of the training, they present their ideas to a "shark tank." If it's a good idea, the foundation will invest. The first class graduated in May 2013, and it was a fantastic success!

This happened because, under God's anointing and direction, I was able to bring those seven men together and charge them to use their God-given gifts to figure out how to create commerce to bless the Messianic Body. To see what we've done, go to *israelfirst.org*.

We build these relationships with our wealthier members to disciple them, not to raise money.

GETTING STARTED IN YOUR CHURCH

Just starting a stewardship curriculum alone will not create permanent change in the culture of your church. As church leaders, you build the culture. There are four important elements to implementing stewardship as a culture in your church.

First, and most important, get the passion and support of the senior pastor behind you. He has to seriously buy into the concept. It can't be something he pushes to the periphery of the church.

Ask him, "What has the Lord put on your heart? What do you want to see financially for your church?"

Get him fired up, and keep him fired up. Bring him to a Generous Giving annual event.

Second, teach and train the staff. Get them behind you. They may be intimidated at first. Walk them through the seven points I listed earlier in this chapter. Show them how each point will benefit them as individuals and as church leaders. Help them develop the vision of a changed, dynamic, prosperous church.

Third, identify and build your stewardship leader team. The staff will help you recruit this team. They know the key people.

Look at having two teams. One will be the launch team. They may not be a good fit for the long-term, but they possess the skills and enthusiasm for getting the ministry off the ground.

Fourth, figure out your demographics according to who in your church is *Struggling, Stable, Solid* and *Surplussed*. The church staff and leadership teams can help refine this.

If you have multiple campuses like Gateway, think about tailoring your stewardship ministry to each campus because each is different socio-economically and demographically. One of our campuses has a higher income level and more married couples than another campus which has 60% single parents.

GATEWAY QUALIFIED KINGDOM ADVISOR PROJECT

Financial professionals in your church are either the best volunteers or the absolute worst. The majority are the best, but the worst, few though they may be, have caused a wall between the church and the financial community.

Say you're a financial professional, but you don't know your pastor well. You offer to help him start a stewardship ministry. The first thing your pastor may be thinking is: *"You're in it to build your business."*

Take the time to get to know him and for him to get to know you. Have heart-to-heart conversations where you share your vision for the church. Help him see the bigger picture. Remember, 70% of pastors don't have a close friend. That may well become one of your primary roles in the church.

Gateway has been running an advisor community since 2006. I know the people in this group very well. I wanted a way to take their qualifications and help people in the church. And I wanted them to be prepared as well because serving the church is different than their normal jobs.

In cooperation with Kingdom Advisors, we took that organization's qualifications and added to them. Gateway Kingdom Advisors take a *Catch the Vision* leadership class which confirms they are a member of the church and agree with our tenets and philosophies.

We check their giving record. They know this up front. Are they giving to the church? *(Where their treasure is, is where their heart is.)*

We take them through a specially designed Advisor Journey of Generosity where I share my heart and learn what God is doing in their lives.

Finally, they have to go through the Kingdom Advisors qualification process and maintain adherence to Kingdom Advisor standards. A few years ago, Kingdom Advisors renewal process and due diligence revealed one of our advisors had been given a lifetime ban from the Security Exchange Commission. I learned the man had major ethical issues. Kingdom Advisors is a tremendous support for us.

These ideas should be enough to get you started. I pray this book has blessed you and stimulated you to dig deeper into Stewardship and Generosity. I hope my words have given you insights and encouragement into how these Biblical concepts apply to your personal life and to your church. The Generous Life can transform your church into a beacon for God in a world that is lost and hurting and seeking answers—answers they won't find in government or anywhere else in the secular world; answers they will only find in God and His Word.

I am excited to see what God is going to build through your ministry!

CONCLUSION

Life can be hard, and the challenges of personal money management don't make it any easier. I caution you to please give yourself and others grace around the subject of money. The God we serve is a loving, gracious and generous God who is conforming us into the image of Christ through trials, tribulation and even in the blessing of His gifts. The key to success in anything we attempt is to never give up. Despite setbacks and heartache, don't give up. You will find success through perseverance and diligence. *Quitting* is not in your vocabulary; it is not an option.

Keep in mind you are not called to perfection, only faithful stewardship.

Those of you who are naturally gifted to manage money, the Body of Christ needs you to stand up and lead. Pour yourself into the Scriptures and get equipped to teach, counsel and disciple others. Submit to your local church authority, and use your Romans 12 gifts of leadership and administration to help your fellow brothers and sisters. The days are short, and people walk in all kinds of bondage, not able to reach their calling. You may be the coach God has placed in their life to help.

At the end of the day, I frequently think about one hundred years from now, how all of us who are alive today will be on the other side of life celebrating victories and sharing stories of God's faithfulness as we lived. Life really is a temporary assignment that impacts eternity; however, today we have the privilege of continuing the story of the book of Acts.

As we walk through this journey, keep the end goal in mind. We all have a part to play as witnesses of Christ. In conclusion, I will leave you with Jesus' final dialog with His disciples.

Acts 1:6–11

Then they gathered around him and asked him, "Lord, are you at this time going to restore the kingdom to Israel?" He said to them: "It is not for you to know the times or dates the Father has set by his own authority. But you will receive power when the Holy Spirit comes on you; and you will be my witnesses in Jerusalem, and in all Judea and Samaria, and to the ends of the earth." After he said this, he was taken up before their very eyes, and a cloud hid him from their sight. They were looking intently up into the sky as he was going, when suddenly two men dressed in white stood beside them. "Men of Galilee," they said, "why do you stand here looking into the sky? This same Jesus, who has been taken from you into heaven, will come back in the same way you have seen him go into heaven."

To echo the words of my Lord Jesus and the angels who followed: "Go in the power of the Holy Spirit," and "What are you doing standing there looking at the sky?"

Get a move on, stewards!

ABOUT THE AUTHOR

In 2002, Gunnar Johnson, a construction worker, was attending a Crown Financial Retreat in Florida. One morning, God told him He was going to use him in full-time ministry to build stewardship ministries across the world in order to set people spiritually and financially free to serve Him.

Gunnar has served as the Executive Pastor of Financial Stewardship at Gateway Church in Southlake, Texas since 2006. A fan of cycling and an avid skate-boarder, he has been happily married to Missy, his high-school sweetheart, since June 1996. They have three children—Faith, Katelyn and Elijah and live in Trophy Club, Texas.

This book is the culmination of over 10 years of faith, struggles and obedience to carry out a very clear and precise vision God gave him on how to build a stewardship ministry. It's the story of how his encounter with God forever changed his life course and taught him how you handle finances is an issue of your heart.

CPSIA information can be obtained at www.ICGtesting.com
Printed in the USA
LVOW01s2030261213

366895LV00002B/2/P

9 780989 516716